THE KLICKITAT INDIANS

THE KLICKITAT INDIANS

BY SELMA NEILS

ILLUSTRATIONS BY GREG HOLLY

Binford & Mort Publishing
Portland, Oregon

The Klickitat Indians

Copyright © 1985 by Selma Neils

Printed in the United States of America

Library of Congress Catalog Card Number: 85-72818
ISBN: 0-8323-0446-8 (softcover)

First Edition 1985

FORWARD

After having lived as a neighbor to many of the Klickitat Indians in the small lumbering town of Klickitat for 39 years, I got to know them well. I gained their friendship and trust and felt the same towards them. No matter how strong the friendship there is a hidden restraint among races, just as there is between ethnic groups.

We fail to give them due respect for the great progress they made in developing their own culture and their adjustment to the ways of the white man. I became filled with the need to tell their stories so that others would come to respect their accomplishments.

Friends felt the same way and were instrumental in searching out stories of the Klickitats and of these there were three without whom it would not have been done. They are Viola Elsner, Sophie Nelson and my daughter, Barbara Street. To them I am most grateful.

Selma M. Neils
April 4, 1985

KLICKITAT COUNTY

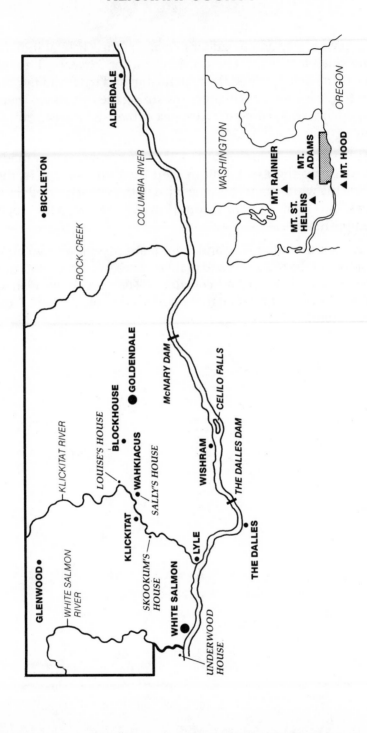

TABLE OF CONTENTS

Geologic Past

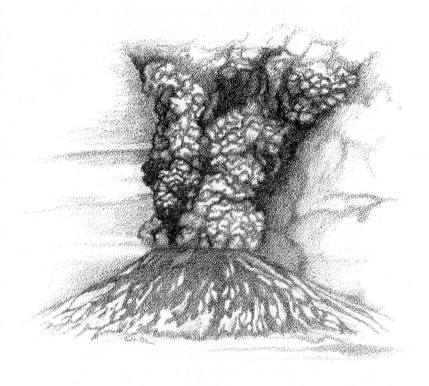

Mount St. Helens, still bringing changes to the Pacific Northwest

Before the first colonial settlements were made here in the United States, the land was occupied by savages, whom several centuries earlier Columbus had given the name of Indians. They claimed the land as theirs made by the Great Spirit for their use alone. But the white man wanted it, and, in fact, had to have some of it to raise food if his settlements were to become permanent. The way this has worked out became a grievous problem and still is so today, needing thought and understanding.

But to become the beautiful land that made homes for the Indians, it went through long ages of geologic turbulences and cataclysmic changes. The part known as the Northwest, in the days of exploration, became the states of Oregon and Washington, along with parts of Idaho, Nevada, Montana, California, and British Columbia.

The man who did the most to bring an awareness of the geologic past was Dr. Thomas Condon. In 1862 the Congregational Church at The Dalles had invited him to be its pastor. It was an ideal place to learn about the mysteries of the past, as his pastoral calls took him into the back country, where he could explore and study the various formations so well exposed in that part of the region. These efforts helped him to become a geologist of wide renown, and helped people to "learn to read the rocks" and gain an appreciation of geologic past.

In the region's early disturbances there were upthrusts from the seas so violent that the sediments of the ocean floor were changed by heat to slate and marble, through which streams of liquid granite were forced. Immense areas were tilted above sea level to heights greater than existing mountains, and great seas were impounded as lakes behind these barriers. Fossils of marine animals mark the ancient shore lines, and long periods of rest allowed the marshy lakes to turn to beds of coal.

The age of mountain uplift ended in the age of fire. Volcanic eruption and seismic forces blew out great flows of lava and ash. Throughout the Columbia Basin the surface is mainly volcanic rock overlaying the shattered fragments of the earth's original crust. This huge lava flow of the Northwest is one of the largest in the world, covering eastern parts of Oregon, and Washington, northern California, and the Snake River plain in Idaho, approximately 250,000 square miles. Most of this lava did not come from volcanic eruptions, but from fissures and blowouts in the earth's crust as the earth cooled and shrank.

Perhaps the most spectacular result of the age of fire was the snow peaks, which are such prominent features of the Northwest. There are still fourteen peaks of 10,000 feet or better in height, with countless lesser peaks, such as Mount St. Helens, which blew its top in May 1980.

Mt. Mazama, though not one of the present peaks, was once the high mountain that blew out its entire core to form a caldera now holding the beautiful two thousand foot deep blue Crater Lake in southern Oregon. While there are other crater lakes in the world, this beautiful lake in its dramatic setting is certainly one of the most scenic. During its formation three small cinder cones rose to blow off the gases of the dying fires, and one cone known as Wizard Island still shows above the surface of the water, leaving a stump of the old volcano to form a sharp rim of one to two thousand feet high around the crater.

Mt. Newberry, another volcano that blew its core, now holds Paulina and East Lakes. It is perhaps best known geologically for the many tree casts that were formed when the lava covered the nearby forests. Today, most visitors are more interested in the lakes, excellent trout fishing and give little thought to the volcanic formation.

In the Three Sisters area, also in the Oregon Cascades, there is evidence of the biggest volcano of all. Here, north of Crater Lake, a circular group of mountains shows that a far greater lake existed. This lake was created by the destruction of the gigantic volcano that has been given the name Mt. Multnomah, an old peak that rose a mile higher than the present summit of the Three Sisters. The explosion that destroyed it left one of the biggest calderas in the world, a circle of fifty young volcanic cones and a lava flow of eighty square miles.

The people of the Northwest have become more interested in volcanoes after Mount St. Helens erupted in May of 1980, sending its mud down the rivers, distributing its ash over the area for miles around, destroying property, and taking many lives. It was once a beautiful landmark, now reduced to a big hill, but its eruption gave people living today a sense of what volcanic activity was like in the past.

In the course of time new forces produced the glacial flows that came down across North America. Most geologists claim there were a number of such flows over a period of time and they left their scars chiefly in two ways, glaciers and floods. Since glacial times, there has been gradual subsidence of the land. The elevation of western America was then higher than it is today, the Willamette Valley was a plateau and Puget Sound was dry.

3

The mouth of the Columbia River and the approach to the Strait of Juan de Fuca were twenty miles farther out to sea.

The glaciers created new systems of drainage and formed new waterways, lakes, and ponds. Even today the Yakima River presents a rare phenomenon as described by Fuller in his *History of the Pacific Northwest* as a stream pursuing its course in apparent disregard of the topography of the country. "The Yakima flows south and passes through at least seven mountain ridges which extend east and west. Some of the ridges are two to three thousand feet high. They are a set of wrinkles in the basalt, caused by the pressure from the south. The reason why the stream did not seek the valleys is that they were there first, and the uplift of the ridges was so slow that the water was able to wear the rock away as fast as it rose above the channel. Thus the ridges continued to grow, each provided with a notch for the river. Seldom have surface movements and erosive action been so precisely matched as to cancel each other over a period of thousands of years."

The Columbia is one of the great rivers of the world. It is 1,264 miles long and its drainage area is 259,000 square miles. One of the unique features of this river is one of its old channels known as the Grand Coulee. This coulee is one of the best examples of canyon cutting by glacial waters and several features entitle it to be considered among the wonders of the world. Flood waters from the melting glaciers found their way down the coulee instead of across country. Long after it had been abandoned by the great river, further glaciation caused it to be reoccupied and new floods poured over the falls. These falls, now dry, have no known competitor as to size, as they were three miles wide and 417 feet high. One cannot fathom the amount of water that accumulated and poured over this precipice, gouging and plowing its way, tearing out canyons and coulees along the rivers to form the scenic gorges that we have today.

All through these years changes in climate took place and left their story in the fossilized bones of many large and strange animals, as well as in many examples of petrified trees and plants. As proof, the author has a piece of petrified cypress hanging on her living room wall, which came from the dirt bank of one of the side canyons of the Klickitat River. A twelve foot stump of sequoia was unearthed during excavation of a logging road near the Klickitat sawmill. Many other specimens have been found that show the area knew a warm and humid climate.

After these periods of turbulence and change there had to be periods of healing, time for the several hundred year old trees to take root and grow, and for grasses to cover the tortured surfaces of lava flows. No human witnesses tell of what was taking place and no one knows when people first came to settle among the scenic wonders of the Northwest. No one is able to tell who the "old people" were who lived here in prehistoric times, where they came from, or when the present-day Indians first made it their home.

Migrations

The cold, hard journey down from the north.

One of the mysteries of history is: when and from where did the Indians come to the Americas. Ethnologists and anthropologists have developed a theory that all the Indians in both Americas came from the same source, and that they came in migrations from Asia, across the Bering Sea on intermittent land bridges that connected Asia and America. Even now the base of entry is less than sixty miles wide, with two stone islands to break distances into shorter steps, which in the geologic past may have been dry or frozen.

They say that as these migrations came, the people gradually found the way down the mountain passes to warmer and more hospitable climates, perhaps as pressure from oncoming migrations forced them to move on. Each group, through the years, developed its own way of life, with food, crafts, and style of shelter depending on the resources of the area in which they settled.

The Plains Indians covered their teepees with skins because the buffalo were plentiful, while the Coast Indians made their homes of cedarwood because cedar was native and could be easily split with stone axes and horn chisels. In the Mid-Columbia region the permanent homes were of cedar planks, while the temporary ones were pole teepees covered with mats of grasses and rushes. It is the portable type of lodge that one thinks of as an Indian home.

The Southwest Indians used many of the rocky cliffs for homes, or covered their shelters with dirt to make the hogan style shelter. These same Indians made their utensils out of pottery because a suitable clay was available. The pots dried in the hot sun served until they learned to bake them in piles of fresh manure where the heat was enough to make them like "kiln dried" pottery.

In the Northwest, along the Columbia River, Indians carved their implements and sculptures of stone, which was available in many colors and textures.

All of the American Indians share a few similar characteristics. They have Mongolian features with straight black hair, black eyes, high cheek bones, and almost beardless faces.

Some authorities find it difficult to accept the theory that all Indians came from a common source, but other theories are equally hard to believe, such as one put forth by a church group that the Indians are descendants of the Lost Tribes of Israel of Biblical times. The real facts may never be ascertained, as many of the sites that hold the answers have been covered by waters of the many dams built along the Columbia River in recent years.

Arrival of Columbus

Christopher Columbus encounters natives inhabiting the Caribbean Islands.

A change of life for the Indians came from contact with the white man.

Columbus, as far as we know, was the first white man to see these early aborigines in the Americas. He came in 1492 from Spain seeking passage to the East Indies for spices, and because he found natives inhabiting these lands, he named them Indians. Finding no route to the Spice Islands and no silver or gold, he took a few natives back to Spain as a proof of what he had found, and there they were a great attraction.

On successive trips Columbus sent more natives to Europe to be sold as slaves. He and other explorers, not finding the expected riches in the New World, made their fortunes from available material. This pattern was followed wherever the Spanish conquered. Florida, the southern United States, and Mexico became a source of Spanish slave trade.

The Spanish continued to send explorers and adventurers to seek out these southern Indian lands. Men like Cortez and Pizarro stole the hoards of gold treasured by the mountain tribes and then massacred the natives through deceit and treachery. To take the gold from the infidels seemed justifiable as long as it was done in the name of God or the King.

It is true that this took place long before the white man had any knowledge of the Northwest Indians and far from them, but it began a pattern of Indian dealings and attitudes which reached down through both space and time.

The Spaniards had brought horses on their ships and some escaped—ten stallions, five mares, and one foal, to become the beginning of the wild horse herds that still are found in parts of the West.

For centuries the Plains Indians had stalked the buffalo on foot, living dangerously or starving while the buffalo multiplied and grew into vast herds. Meantime, the wild horse herds increased until the Indians were able to capture some of the animals for their own use.

This widened their range of activity in buffalo hunting, and carried them into other tribal lands. As the Indians' ability in the hunt grew, the buffalo herds began to diminish as they were the Indians' staple source of food. The Indians became more nomadic and more hostile to trespassers which ended in more tribal warfare.

One is apt to forget how recent was the first contact with the whites. It moved slowly across the continent and brought many changes down through the years. Some of the changes brought betterment, while others, like insidious cancers, brought suffering and deterioration.

In their early days the Indians had to live near their sources of food as their only transportation was by foot. Game and fish from forest and streams were heavy and it was the duty of the squaws to be the burden bearers who at times had the help of dogs, but a large dog could carry only fifty pounds. The mountains and fields furnished berries and bulbs. It all had to be worked for, and for the women it was not the glamorous life of which Indian romances tell. Their food, clothing, and shelter had to be secured from nature, and nature was not always bountiful.

The different tribes have different physiques depending on their mode of life. Coast Indians, for example, had short legs, well bowed, from constantly squatting in a canoe. They all have brown skins, but of different hues, and features depend on the genes of their local tribesmen. Why they were called redskins, no one seems to know.

One can scarcely realize how different life became for the Indians who lived in the Mid-Columbia area when they obtained horses from the tribes farther east around 1750. They still gathered their variety of foods in family groups, but they did not have to carry the fish, the game, the bulbs, and the berries. In spite of this, horses were not plentiful because they had to be acquired through raid or trade.

These Mid-Columbian Indians were indeed fortunate for they had the great fisheries of the Columbia and the huckleberry fields on the shoulders of Mount Adams from which to garner food to be used for trading for less available food and horses. They also harvested cedar roots, squaw grass, and rushes for baskets which were good trade items, and so they built up a trading center known over the whole Northwest.

IV

Explorations

Captain Robert Gray's ship, the "Columbia," was the first to sail up the river named in its' honor.

Knowledge of the Pacific Coast was growing as explorers of Spain, Portugal, Russia, England, and America traveled the Pacific waters along the American coast looking for that elusive passage that they expected to find through the American Continent that would give them a shorter route to the East Indies. All coastal explorations meant contact with the Indians, as the ships needed to fill their water casks or pick up a few furs in trade. They found no gold or silver, but they learned the value of the herds of sea otter to be found along the coast. These animals have some of the softest fur in the world which was in such demand on the Canton market that a single prime skin sold for a hundred dollars. Finding no precious metals, the competitors for this elegant fur became ruthless in their efforts to get the Indians to trade.

The march of world events warned the Spanish that if they were to have a part of this Pacific Coast, they would have to take renewed action. To Spain's good fortune, France, England, and American colonies became involved in the Revolutionary War, leaving Spain in a favorable position to make settlements at San Diego and Monterey and begin their line of missions. They were interested in Christianizing the natives and improving their living conditions, but the sea otter were plentiful on the California coast and the Spanish lust for gold no doubt increased their missionary zeal.

Before this, Russia had sent Vitus Bering out to explore in 1741, but things moved slowly in those northern waters, and it was not until 1771 that they sent out their first shipment of furs direct from Kamchatka to Canton. A permanent settlement was made at Sitka, with the ruthless Baranoff as Governor. Later the Russians established a fort and farm just north of San Francisco Bay to raise supplies for the northern posts.

The English had been busy with their troubles in the American colonies and were a little slow in getting to the Northwest coast, even though the different adventurers met at Canton, where Cook's men had been first to sell their furs profitably in 1779. There were British vessels trading along the coast.

The great English navigator, Cook, passed and repassed the vicinity of the Columbia and the opening to the Straits of Juan de Fuca without finding either, but in 1779 the crew took with them a quantity of furs to China where the demand was great. Gold, silver and jewels had eluded them, but the high prices received from the furs opened their eyes to the fact that they had something as good as gold.

In the beginning Indians received only trinkets or cheap baubles in trade, and they were badly cheated. But they were not stupid and soon learned that they could get the things they prized, such as iron, guns, blankets, copper, brass kettles, and things they could use and wear. These articles were not only labor savers but they gave prestige to the owner among his fellow tribesmen. Just think of what it meant for a squaw to have a kettle in which to cook instead of heating rocks to cook in a basket; or what it did to her ego to wrap herself in a colorful blanket instead of a drab tule mat; or what it did for a buck who could get more game with a new gun than his neighbor could with a bow and arrow.

Despite the journeys of many explorers, who followed the usual practice of laying claim to everything in sight and even what they imagined to be in the distance, and demanding the whole coast by priority of discovery, the Columbia River had not been found. Lyman in his "Columbia River" tells of the voyage that changed the lives of all of us, white and Indian alike, even down to the present day.

"Gray sailed south on May 10, 1792, passed abreast of the same reflex of water, where, nine days before, he had tried vainly to enter. The morning of the 11th dawned clear and favorable, light wind, gentle sea, a broad channel, plainly sufficient depths. The time had now come. The man and the occasion met. Gray seems to have been ready to take some chances for the sake of success. He always hugged the shore closely, enough to be on intimate terms with it. And he was ready to seize and use favorable circumstances, so, laconically stated in his log book, he ran in with full sail and at ten o'clock found himself in a large river of fresh water at a point twenty miles from the coast."

The next day, he went fifteen miles farther upstream. Natives in canoes thronged around the ship and were apparently friendly. Gray planted an American flag, the Stars and Stripes, and took possession of the land for the United States. He named the river "Columbia" after his ship. A large quantity of furs was secured and relations were good. The great exploit was complete, and the long sought for river had been found by an American. During this time, interest was great in gaining control of this land, as claims to the interior were important. To establish such British claims, a small party of Scots and Canadians under the leadership of Alexander MacKenzie came across Canada and after wide exploration reached the Pacific Ocean at 52 degrees, 24 minutes, and 48 seconds, where the leader wrote on a rock, still preserved, with vermillion and grease, "Alexander Mac-Kenzie from Canada by land, July 22, 1791."

It was a remarkable feat and MacKenzie was a remarkable man to accomplish it. At first glance, it seems to have been too far north to have any influence on the Klickitat Indians down on the middle Columbia, but because such news always spread and aroused new interest, Thomas Jefferson was spurred on when he became President to organize what became known as the Lewis and Clark Expedition. The fur companies also became further interested in westward expansion.

V

Lewis and Clark

Meriwether Lewis and William Clark were commissioned by Congress and President Jefferson to lead a group to travel to the west to gain information about the land, its mineral wealth, its climate and soils, its animals and plants, its Indians, and the trade possibilities. It was hoped this would lay a basis for dealing with the Indian question itself, as it had been a problem ever since the time of Columbus, and it was hoped that an ethical solution could be found.

The expedition's task had been slightly simplified just before it left, when the United States acquired from France in 1803 the area that became known as the Louisiana Territory for $1,500,000, which included "all the waters of the Mississippi and Missouri," thus more than doubling the area of the United States. This would give the expedition greater freedom in dealing with the Indians by getting the French out of the area, but the British were still there, and friendly to the Indians, while working their fur trade westward.

It was a big responsibility for this crew under the leadership of these two able men, who were both seasoned army captains and campaigners. Clark and Lewis were to exercise equal authority. They entered the Missouri on May 14, 1804, and after learning to adjust to each other and the wilderness, they wintered near the Mandan Villages. They had a crew of twenty-five; the hunter and interpreter Drouiliard; the interpreter Charbonneau and his Indian wife, Sacajawea, and her newborn baby boy; Clark's black slave, York; the two captains; and Lewis's dog, Scammon. It was said that the presence of a woman and child would show that they were on a mission of peace.

It was a journey of many experiences and the gathering of much information, with some of the men as well as the captains keeping daily journals. Sacajawea is credited with helping them get needed horses from the Shoshones, as her brother, Cameawait, was one of the chiefs of that tribe. She had been stolen as a child and held until bought or won in a gambling game by Charbonneau, who had two other wives at the time.

Clark insisted they go through the marriage ceremony before they set out on the journey. Her husband, an older man and French Canadian, had lived around the Mandans for many years, earning a living with trapping for furs or acting as a guide and interpreter to trapping parties. His knowledge of Indian languages was not as good as he pretended, and as a result, he sometimes made serious blunders. One of these was his interesting interpretation of the name of Sacajawea, which really meant boat or canoe launcher instead of "Bird Woman." When Charbonneau attempted to tell the meaning of the word by Indian signs, in his self-important way, he made signs of flying using motions of his arms at shoulder height which were understood as the flight of a bird. The proper signs for the Shoshone name, Sacajawea, should have been made with the arms and hands at the waistline to indicate the motion of one who propels a boat, thus giving the name of boat or canoe launcher.

He was a loutish fellow, and was given to striking his wife. Clark objected severely to this and promised him real punishment if he continued. Many authors have written of Sacajawea making a great romance of her regard for Clark, but how could any woman, red or white, not have had deep affection for a man well groomed, kind, and thoughtful of her. She proved to be of great help, because she knew herbs and plants which could be used in their diets and as medicines. She also made moccasins and kept the clothing in repair. One must marvel at this young Indian girl who could care for a little child on a trip that had hardships that were almost more than the men could bear.

They had no doctors in the crew, and while not versed in medicine, they treated illnesses and injuries chiefly with salts and barks, and though one man died from natural causes shortly after leaving St. Louis, they did well with the men's accidents and stomach upsets from eating strange or contaminated food. As mentioned in the journals, on the return journey Sacajawea gathered fennel from which she made tea to treat stomach disorders.

Not all contacts with Indians were friendly, but they were able to maintain control of the situation; Indian men were anxious to see how the guns worked and what they could accomplish, and the Indian women were curious about the clothing and preparation of food. It was natural for this interest to lead to desire, and if they had nothing to trade, it led to thievery.

The expedition reported that the tribes were of different physiques and dispositions. They were interested to find that the Blackfeet had feet no dirtier than others and that the Flatheads did not have flat heads, but they did find a tribe near the mouth of the Columbia River which practiced flattening the heads of their upper class, never of their slaves.

By the time they reached Walla Walla, they had heard of the rough water and long portages that lay ahead. Here they met Chief Yel-lep-pit, a very friendly man from whom they were able to get fresh fish and roots. In return they gave him a medal and a small American flag, which pleased him greatly. He was about five feet eight inches in height and well liked by his people. Here they saw pierced noses and men wearing a bead or shell in the nose.

The custom of giving medals to prominent red men was a custom of long standing. The Spanish, the French, the English, and the Dutch had done it in the Colonies long before there was a United States, and the Indians who were so honored set remarkable store by them. The medal became an important part of a leader's ceremonial dress; to the owner it was a powerful medicine amulet from the white man, who realized what a great person the Indian really was. Lewis and Clark gave four such medals along the Columbia and two have been recovered and given to the Museum at Maryhill.

Lewis and Clark were not surprised to find many Indians in the strategic narrows of the Columbia, but they found many more than they had expected. This was the part of the river about which they had been hearing, where the mile-wide river entered a hundred foot funnel of tumbling cataracts. The water was confined by slabs of basalt and was of two hundred feet or more in depth with some unfathomable holes that resulted in swirls and eddies with great whirlpools in the rushing waters. After reconnoitering, the canoes were lightened of the men who could not swim and of some of the most precious supplies. Men were stationed with ropes to throw out to victims in case of trouble, and careful watch was kept over the baggage. The Indians crowded to the rocks below to salvage for themselves any wreckage as booty. Miraculously, the boats came through only slightly damaged. These waters are now covered by the backwater from The Dalles Dam.

The portages with the heavy boats were especially trying, as the rocks were covered with dried grass and fish skins and all the rest of the debris of Indian living, and all infested with swarms of fleas. The men worked naked so as to more easily free themselves of the pests. All this while, constant vigilance had to be kept on their belongings to guard them against the pilfering habits of these Indians.

Many of the Indians were from other bands and even other tribes, who were trying to get their winter supply of fish from the late run of salmon. These hazardous waters were the great trading center of the Northwest. Here natives came from as far as the ocean shores, even from beyond the shining rocky mountains, and from the hinterlands to the north and south. It was the place to learn how other tribes lived, and even a wider field from which to choose a wife.

Even at this late season they had not all returned to their homes, but were living in temporary mat shelters, until soon the winter winds would get too cold and they would leave. But there were permanent homes sheltering those who called this place, known as Wishram, their home.

This is how Captain Clark described what he saw on October 24, 1805. "A village of twenty wood houses in a deep bend of the Star'd Side below which a rugid black rock about 20' hiter (sic) than the Common high flood of the river...The natives of the village—One of whom invited me into his home which I found to be large and commodious, and the first wooden houses, in which I have been, Since we left those in the vicinity of Ollinois, they were scattered promiscuously on an elevated situation near a mound some thirty feet above the common level which mound has every evidence of being artificial."

They made no further mention of the mound, which is, no doubt, the one that later became known as Wakemap, holding its treasures until the 1920's when it was scientifically excavated to reveal many of its secrets of the past. It, too, has been covered by the backwaters of The Dalles Dam.

Lewis and Clark reported the Indians of the Mid-Columbia area were of good physique, taller than most, with aquiline features and small hands and feet. The women were sometimes beautiful when young, but tended to become corpulent with age. One thing they noticed was that their teeth were worn down, some right down to the gums. They decided this must come from the constant blowing sand. The fish were prepared and dried in the open and in the process it was dusted with sand. Such a constant diet slowly ground down the teeth no less than the dentist's tool that is used today. They were also troubled with sore eyes, no doubt caused by the irritations of blowing sand and the constant smoke from the daily cooking fires in their houses.

The Indians called the wind "the ever talking wind." Through the gorge the wind is pretty constant, and especially in the narrows, it funnels down with real vigor. In the preparation of fish, which was the main source of food, the wind was a great help in drying the fish. The men caught the fish, by spear or nets, and the women prepared them by skinning, cleaning, and cutting them into strips in prescribed ways. This was important, according to their rituals, in order to keep the fish coming upstream. They were then laid on rocks or built-up racks to dry in the sun and wind. The fish were turned regularly, and if the process went too slowly, they were hung in smoke from alder fires. All this while the gorge wind peppered the fish with fine sand, which was constantly on the move. The fish was then pounded to a powdery meal, and for winter use it was stored in grass baskets one foot in diameter and two feet long, which had been carefully lined with roasted salmon skins, skin side out, covered with more skins, and sewed shut. One such basket held ninety to one hundred pounds of powdered fish. Clark mentions seeing these baskets piled in stacks like cordwood with seven in a row and five set on top and the whole stack covered with more mats. If piled in a dry spot, such prepared fish could last for several years in good condition.

They reported these Indians in the narrows as "filthy and flea ridden." But could they be anything but dirty and pest infested with all these numbers living in this rocky defile with no sanitation and no refrigeration? Insect pests are not easily gotten rid of even with modern chemicals, and the Indians did not even have soap. Most of us have learned how smelly one over-ripe fish can get. Here it wasn't a question of being fastidious; it was a question of a livelihood. Clark called one squaw "a dirty old bitch" when she didn't want to get out of his way. No doubt, she felt that she was there first.

The Lewis and Clark camp was made at the present site of The Dalles, on an easily defended point of land, south of what is now called Mill Creek. Constant watch was kept to prevent attack. There were small groups of Indian huts on both sides of the river seemingly independent of each other, some of planks and some of mats, built low in the ground with few openings. Lewis and Clark traded for some salmon, but the supply was limited, as this was the natives' winter food.

Here in the Mid-Columbia the Indians had not been surprised to see the white men as they had come and gone, for they, no doubt, had heard of the white men by their own system of "telegraph" from Walla Walla. They must have heard of the white men who had come to their shores in big "white winged canoes," for there was evidence of trade goods. Clark reported seeing one blue and two scarlet blankets, seamen's clothing, a gun, and a brass kettle. Even in the burial vaults that they had seen along the river there had been a brass kettle and a frying pan that had been "killed," which meant that they had been made unfit for use so as to accompany their owners to the Spirit World where everything would be made whole.

While the Indians were not surprised, they were certainly curious. The men wanted to handle the guns and see how they worked, and the women wanted to investigate the clothing to see how they were fashioned and the materials of which they were made. The white men's meals and methods of cooking made the Indians so curious that it was hard to keep them out of the cooking pots and bales.

They were all interested in York, Clark's Negro slave, and he had a hard time convincing them that his skin was really black and not painted. They tried rubbing, and even washing, until they believed that he was really black.

On the way down river they passed Memaloose Island, which for generations, perhaps for centuries, had been an Indian burial ground, there were several more burial islands that the Indians used because they were isolated from wild animals. Here wooden shelters had been built and the dead, wrapped in blankets, were laid on shelves or set on benches until they were pushed aside as bundles of bones to make way for the next ones. Beads, arrows, and special possessions were buried with them for their future use. The plank doors were shut and sealed with dirt and rocks. Indians did not visit these graves except for burial or to redress their relatives in new blankets.

The portage at the Cascades was made without mishap, but the Indians were becoming more thievish, and many were armed with pistols, muskets, and powder flasks. From there, Lewis and Clark went on down to the ocean and wintered in make-shift shelters that they called Fort Clatsop, where they had dealings with the Chinook Indians. It was here they found that the Indians of the upper class flattened the heads of the new-born children with a device tied to the forehead which made the head become slanted from the brows to the top of the head. It seemed to give no pain nor change their mentality, but they thought it made them beautiful.

It was a rainy winter, no ships came in to trade, and the men were constantly wet from hunting in the wet forests and brush. In their limited quarters there was no way to dry their clothing. There was much sickness and discomfort, and they had trouble keeping their game long enough to make proper use of it. Elk was the chief game, and as winter came on, they had to go farther inland to get it. They needed a considerable amount as meat was their chief food and they were heavy eaters. They built a salt cairn, where they made salt from sea water for their present needs and their journey home. This site is still preserved as a historic site at Seaside, Oregon. Blubber and whale oil were procured from the Indians, as a whale had washed ashore not far from their camp.

They made more than four hundred pair of moccasins and other clothing from the skins of the game that they had shot, and they prepared in every way they could for the long trip home. They were glad to leave on March 21, 1806, having had just six days of sunshine all winter.

On the trip up river, they found the Indians had grown more sullen. For them, too, food supplies had run low in early spring, and they had become more thievish, keeping the explorers constantly on the defensive. They had found villages at the mouths of both the White Salmon and Klickitat rivers. Here on the return journey they noticed that one house, which formerly had stood on a bluff above the gorge, had been moved a short distance and the men wondered if that was a result of spring house-cleaning or a way to get rid of swarms of fleas.

The Expedition reached St. Louis on September 23, 1806. They had left Coulter, who later discovered Yellowstone, and Charbonneau and Sacajawea at the Mandan Villages. They had kept careful notes and so had several of the men. The first of these records was published in 1807, but the Captains did not publish their own journals until some years later, and they have since gone through many editions. Clark reported that he had paid off Charbonneau and offered to be of service to him if he came to St. Louis. He offered to adopt Baptiste, their son, and to educate him, which he later did. He called him Pomp, which in Shoshone meant first, and "my dancing boy" as little Baptiste would shuffle to the music of violins, clinging to Sacajawea's hand, and, as he grew a little older, he would dance with the men as they went through their nightly routine for the Indians.

The expedition's visit could not but have an influence on the Indians, and while they may not have been surprised, changes came into their lives because of the trade goods and seeing what the trade goods could do. It did not only change customs, but affected perceptions as well. Bernard de Voto in his *Course of Empire* said, "It is not within my province to determine whether or how far Lewis and Clark shared the evening pleasures of the men which the records freely record. The folklore may be mentioned, however, and there is a lot of it. The West is still stocked with people who claim to have been descended from Lewis and women of most tribes the Expedition met, and they are not unknown in the East. I have corresponded with gentlemen in Virginia and Florida who have elaborate genealogical charts, which convince them, and have talked with a number of professed descendents in the west. Curiously, I have met no one who claims Clark as an ancestor. But literature long ago filled that gap, bestowing on him a love affair with Sacajawea which, on no evidence, has gained ground, even in histories."

So had passed the first known white influence that had come to these Mid-Columbia Indians, the Klickitats.

VI

Pictographs and Petroglyphs

Tsagaglalal, "She who watches."

Time veils the history of the early life of these American Indians, as they left no written records. Early adventurers made little effort to learn of their beginnings, but here in the Pacific Northwest the Early People did leave pictographs, petroglyphs, and stone sculptures to tell a story, if we could only read it.

Pictographs are paintings made on the smooth cleavage surfaces found in basaltic rocks, with natural pigments, which the Indians had learned to use through the years, such as vermillion, ochre, iron oxide, clay, and mineral muds. Some of the pigments had to be burned and powdered, some ground and mixed with mud, some soaked in water. They were then mixed with grease so they could be applied. The pictures are of faces, animals, lines, and figures. Weathering has caused these pigments to fuse with the rock until they are as much a part of the rock as the decorations on china become a part of the whole when fused by kiln firing.

Petroglyphs are prehistoric carvings made by ancient peoples with crude primitive tools of bone or stone on hard basalt surfaces and many are found along the Columbia or other waterways. They are of people, animals, stars, suns, and lines. None of the living Indians have any knowledge of what they meant or of who made them. A few were made with more modern tools and some even show horses, so these had to have been made since the early 1700's when horses were first introduced. When questioned, present-day Indians will simply shrug and say "made by the old people." Petroglyphs usually are found high on the cliffs, but at Roosevelt, they were scattered on the ground, and near old Wishram there was a well decorated mile-long canyon that became known as Petroglyph Canyon.

Perhaps the best known large carving, almost six feet across, is not far from Wishram. The Indians call this carving "Tsagaglalal," which means, "She who watches." The Indian bucks used to tell the maidens that she watched to see if they were faithful. Another is in a sheltered cove near Goldendale, a painting of a group of warriors looking down from a smooth cliff. One can easily climb up to see and touch these pictured heads and find the colors are now an integral part of the rock. The reds, yellows, blacks, and whites will, no doubt, last as long as the rock itself. It gives one an eerie feeling to come upon such a message from the past. One wonders what message someone was trying to tell. Were these braves killed here while trying to defend their nearby village? Were they setting out on a horse stealing raid? It is doubtful their story will ever be told although the sciences of ethnography and paleontology may tell us much in unraveling the past.

When it was learned that the back waters of The Dalles Dam would cover many of the early prehistoric pictographs and petroglyphs, many were removed by scientists who had become interested in preserving as much as they could for future study, and much is now in museums and the Oregon Historical Society.

No work was done on them in the early days, but it was left for later times when it was learned that there was much knowledge to be gained from such excavations, if properly done. Separate pieces of sculptured rock are found in many places, some from prehistoric times and some relatively new, although few, if any, have been made by the present dwellers since their contact with the white man. It is common to find primitive tools and implements made from bone or stone, but it is unusual to find them embellished with additional carvings, which add no efficiency in their use. Additional decorations, however, may have added spiritual or esoteric value. Most pieces found here on the Columbia River show a style and technique that could only come from long tradition. The circled eye and the definite rib cage are common in the Klickitat region. Many were originally painted, and bits of color still cling to some pieces. Red, black, and white, with red the favorite, are the colors found.

Representations are human, animal, and bird, as well as geometric and abstract forms, with a diversity of styles and types. The owl must have been a favorite subject and is referred to as the Spedis Owl, as many have been found made of different rocks and colors. While it is impossible at this time to date the sculptures, it is felt that they were made before the coming of the whites. The Indians now living have no knowledge of their significance or who made them or why. There is no reference to them in their myths or legends.

They say, "Gold is where you find it," and so it is with sculpture. One small piece was found on High Prairie while the seeker was looking for agates in a plowed field above Wahkiacus in a spot far from any known Indian camp or any similar stone outcroppings. It is about the size of a fist and represents a face with the circled eye and with practice marks on the back. Such an unexpected find fills one with emotional conjectures about its past.

In 1964 an important project was carried out by Malcolm and Louise Loring, who volunteered to undertake locating, photographing, sketching, and cataloging the pictographs and petroglyphs in Oregon. These records are now in the Oregon Historical Society in Portland. The Lorings report finding in Oregon alone one hundred twenty-five groups and three hundred forty-five designs, most of which are now under water.

Because the Indians had no written language, the myths, legends, and tales of the past were passed from generation to generation by the storytellers. These were usually the grandfathers who would entertain the family during the long dark winter evenings. It is said that where there is no written language, story-telling becomes recognized as a great accomplishment. The story tellers take pride in memorizing and repeating the old stories, honing and perfecting them until the tales become things of poetic beauty. A chief often would tell the story of heroes of the past to work up the patriotic fervor of his braves when about to go into battle. Many of these tales have been preserved, and ethnologists have a way of deciphering the relationship and movements of the different tribes as passed down by the tales that were memorized by the storytellers.

VII

Mid-Columbia Indians

A fisherman catching salmon from his allotted spot at Celilo Falls.

In earliest times the Northwest Indians lived in an amalgam of Indians, with tribal life developed from the groups of families and clans into bands and then tribes. Ethnologists classified these later tribes, which descended from the ancient migrations, according to the languages they spoke. Linguistic cousins may differ widely in cultural ways and live on no better terms than ordinary families. Their languages may have changed so that they have no understanding of each other's speech, and even though linguistic cousins may differ, yet so stubborn is the construction of language that careful study of it can establish relationships and vaguely make out the lines of an unwritten history beyond the knowledge found in the oldest traditions. Here in this empire of the Columbia three linguistic stocks prevailed: The Shoshean in southwest Oregon; the Sahaptin of southern Washington, northern Oregon, and central Idaho; and Salish in northern Washington, interior British Columbia, northern Idaho, and western Montana. Within each area are many separate tribes, speaking their own languages and having their own mode of life, with different food supplies and means of housing and transportation largely dependent upon local conditions, yet they show their relationships through their language structures.

The Indians had felt the whole land was for their use and they could roam as they pleased unless contested by the prior use of some other band. Some old tales tell that the Klickitats had once lived further east, but the Cayuses had chased them out. Be that as it may, the old Klickitats knew of no such event, but hated the fierce Cayuses as did many other tribes. It was only after the coming of the whites that the boundary lines were drawn more exactly by the Indians themselves.

In the Mid-Columbia region lived a tribe of Indians belonging to the Sahaptin linguistic group who became known as Klickitats. These Indians were fortunate to live in an area where food was relatively plentiful. They lived along the Columbia and the rivers branching from it to the north such as the Lewis, White Salmon, and Klickitat, and as far north as Mt. Adams. They claimed fishing rights on the Columbia to the Cascades and as far up as the John Day River. Long before Lewis and Clark passed here, the fishing rights on the Columbia were passed from father to son. The most desirable spots were usually held by the most powerful families, while less important families held the less productive spots. The reserved fishing spots could only be used by the other Indians if the claimant gave special permission or was absent.

The narrows at The Dalles was the best fishing area, and even among the Indians it was felt that these fish were the best obtainable. Perhaps this was because these were spring-run salmon, able to pass there while still in prime condition.

Because so many Indians congregated here for fishing, it became one of the best trading places in the whole Northwest. They became shrewd traders, using their surplus fish to bargain for articles from distant places. In the old middens, household refuse piles of the past, have been found remnants of buffalo robes, raw iron, and pipe-stone, a red rock from Minnesota so much favored for calumets or peace pipes.

It was the man who hunted and fished, and he was the one who had the fun, racing and gambling, while it was the woman who did the food preparation, the root digging, the berry picking, the basket making, child raising, moving, and providing fuel. Because living was relatively easy, the men rode and roamed. They became the best riders and hunters in the land. They must have had good diets for a goodly number lived to be more than one hundred years old.

After the visit of Lewis and Clark things went along rather quietly until there came renewed contact with the white man, and this was the coming of the fur traders.

VIII

Fur Traders

Beaver pelts were in demand for the manufacture of men's hats.

Captain James Cook is generally credited with establishing the fur industry in 1776 when on a voyage of exploration. His men casually obtained sea otter skins on the Oregon Coast and sold them in China for fabulous prices. The British were the next to become interested, as they had long been active in the fur trade in eastern Canada and the midwest. The Hudson's Bay Company had been chartered by King Charles II of England in 1678. At that time no one understood how vast and rich was the territory covered by the charter nor how absolute were the powers granted. Rival traders were soon forbidden to deal with the Indians at any but designated spots, and this led these traders to organize a rival company in 1783 known as the Northwest Company.

The Indians who had brought the first furs to the ships were bringing less and less as through the years the sea otter herds were diminishing, and now it was the beaver pelts that were in such demand. This was because of men's world style for "plug hats." The best hats were made of felt made from beaver fur. This is due to a peculiarity of the beaver fur, which is comprised of two kinds of hair, one close set, silky and gray; the other coarser, longer and reddish brown (guard hairs). The hair of the soft fur has tiny barblets along its length, which when processed into felt, interlock into a firm mat that makes a stronger but softer felt.

The beaver lived inland along the smaller streams, and the trappers who hunted them broke the trails that opened the West. They were a special breed of men, who were willing to go through great hardship, but they wanted and expected to get rich. They scoured every stream and thus got to meet all the Indians, who seemed to feel no animosity toward them as they did not disturb the land, toward which the Indians held this special feeling of reverence. This was the land the Creator had given them for their use.

Most of the trappers bought Indian wives as a convenience. It was good to get a prepared meal and have their shirts and moccasins made. When they moved on, they had no conscience pangs over leaving the wife or family.

In New York a shrewd merchant named John Jacob Astor, who had been trading for furs along the Canadian border, decided the thing to do was to set up a fur trading post at the mouth of the Columbia, so that furs could be easily picked up and shipped to New York or China, while having the hinterland to draw from. He proceeded to that by sending one crew around Cape Horn in the ship, Tonquin, and for safety's sake another group overland. The Tonquin reached the mouth of the Columbia, but lost eight of the men sent out to reconnoiter the dangerous river bar. Construction of the post was begun on April 10, 1811, giving Americans the first foothold on land in the west. The ship,

Tonquin, went up the coast to trade for furs, and perhaps because it was unwisely captained, the ship was lost and the entire crew massacred.

During this time there was bitter feeling in Canada between The Hudson's Bay Company and the Northwest Company, as both companies knew they had to expand to the west because the old areas were being depleted of game.

The Northwest Company sent out one of their explorers by the name of David Thompson, who had entered their service in 1797. It was he who established the first trading posts in Oregon country just prior to the beginning of Astoria, but they were on the upper Columbia, the Kootenai, the Pend d'Oreille, and other northern streams. He visited all the tribes and set up trading relations in 1810, gaining the friendship of local Indians by providing them with guns and teaching them how to use them against the hostile Blackfeet, who were already armed.

David Thompson had brought his halfbreed wife and three small children to live on Lake Windermere near the headwaters of the Columbia. This is a beautiful scenic area, but one wonders at the resourcefulness of a young mother who could care for a family in such primitive circumstances. No doubt, her Indian heritage was what pulled them through the long cold winters. This brought a new element into the picture and that was permanent settlement.

It was Thompson who did much to bring about the settlement of the West. He was an expert cartographer and his maps are still in use today. He would go on yet another trip of exploration, using Iroquois or halfbreed paddlers, while his wife had to manage alone with a couple of Indian servants.

After exploring most of the northern streams, in the summer of 1811 he set out down the Columbia with the idea of setting up a post near the mouth of the river. The Columbia has a tricky beginning as it flows north for a couple hundred miles before turning around the Selkirk Mountains and heading south. He had already explored the Kootenai, which flows half a mile from the Columbia but heads south and east.

Upon reaching the Snake he was disappointed to find that the Lewis and Clark Expedition had been there before him, which he realized when he was met by the same friendly Chief Yel-le-Pit who was wearing the medal of 1801 that Clark had given him and displaying the small American flag. Here Thompson set up a pole on which he tied a paper bearing the following inscription, which was later found by the first Astorian trading party:

"Know hereby that this country is claimed by Great Britain as part of its territories, and that the Northwest Company of Merchants from Canada, finding the factory for these people inconvenient for them, do hereby intend to erect a factory for the commerce of the country around. D. Thompson. Juncture of the Shawpatin River with the Columbia. July 9, 1811."

He continued downstream. At his camp opposite the mouth of the John Day he was again disappointed to hear that the Americans had established a post, named Astoria, three months earlier. He continued without difficulty and arrived there on July 15, 1811, after coming all the way down the Columbia.

Astoria had been having difficulties. They finally heard that their ship, the Tonquin, and its crew had been lost, leaving them short of some necessary supplies and trade goods. The land party had not yet come. The Indians were reluctant to trade. So Duncan McDougall, now in charge, but not wise in the ways of Indian trading, foolishly showed the Indians a corked empty whiskey jug, telling them that it contained the white man's sicknesses that were so fatal to them. Unless they brought furs, he would uncork the bottle. This threat seemed smart to him, and it did bring more furs, but also it brought much trouble later, when epidemics broke out. The Indians remembered.

Thompson was given a welcome by McDougall, but he stayed only a few days, and when questioned about the interior and chances for trade, he painted a gloomy picture of hostile Indians and scarcity of furs. He told McDougall that the Northwest Company was considering abandoning the territory west of the mountains and there would be no competition for Hudson's Bay Company if they agreed not to infringe on Northwest Company trade. It was true that this area east of the Cascades had little game in the desert areas, but the Astorians felt that Thompson was trying to pull the wool over their eyes.

Astoria never had any trouble in getting young men to come as clerks on the venture called "scribbling clerks" by Washington Irving, the author, when describing Astoria. Among them were Cox, Ross, and Franchere, who wrote of their experiences after they had returned to their former homes. They give us much of interest about the lives of the Indians, but it is regretful that they did not write sooner, for their remembrances may not always be as accurate as could be wished. Others, like Stuart and McKenzie, who did not record their memories, should have, as the latter, especially, had an unusual way of getting along with the natives. To him they were always friendly. He had a way of keeping everything under control and was always attentive to the children, giving them small gifts and patting them on the head. This impressed the Indians.

Robert Stuart and Alexander Ross with their crews started up the river with Thompson on his return trip, but by the time they reached The Dalles, he had outdistanced them. They learned he had a superior boat and, more important, an able and experienced crew of paddlers. They were on their way to set up a post up river, preferably at Okanagan.

Thompson went back to complete some more explorations and surveys. In return for beaver and provisions of dried meat he supplied the Flatheads with their guns. These Indians, long persecuted by the Blackfeet, who already had white men's guns, gave a Blackfeet band the surprise of their lives by opening fire on them with "Lightning Sticks."

Thompson's discoveries and surveys gave the world new knowledge of the northwestern part of the continent through their use by Hudson's Bay Company, but professional cartographers and engineers failed to acknowledge their source, wanting to take the credit themselves. Consequently, people in later years were not aware that Thompson had authored their maps. His records were not published and no one knew what he had accomplished or where he had been until after his death in 1857, poor, blind, unknown, buried in an unmarked grave. As often happens, he was honored a quarter century after his death. He had received no recognition during his lifetime, yet he was one of the greatest explorers of the New World and is now acclaimed as one of the greatest geographers ever produced by English speaking people. In this western country, the North-westerners followed the routes he had laid out and filled the posts he had established. His maps are used to this day.

Thompson's wife had followed him through the years, and she survived him by only three months. Through all the physical hardships, they had raised seven daughters and six sons.

The Astorians continued to have problems, although they did set up Fort Okanagan and other posts under Robert Stuart and Alexander Ross. Cox tells of supplies that they brought with them up river. They consisted of the following:

"The lading was made up of guns and ammunition, spears, knives, hatchets, beaver traps, copper and brass kettles, white and green blankets, rings, thimbles, blue, green, and red cloths, calicoes, beads, hawk bells and for provisions, they carried beef, port, flour, rice, biscuits, tea, sugar, with a moderate quantity of rum and wine."

Meanwhile the Astor overland party began straggling in after torture, starvation, cold treacherous streams, and rugged terrain. The scribbling clerks interviewed them as they reached Astoria and recorded tales of unbelievable suffering, hardship, and death.

Much has been made of the experiences of Sacajawea, and that is as it should be, but the story of Madame Dorion and her fortitude needs to be given more prominence. She was the Iowa Indian wife of Pierre Dorion, the halfbreed Indian interpreter for the Astorian land party under the leadership of William P. Hunt. It is the story of hardship, little food, and winter cold. By the 30th of December they had reached the lovely valley of the Grand Ronde where in the early morning, Madame Dorion gave birth to a child. "Dorion, her husband, remained in camp with her for a day then rejoined us on the 31st," Hunt recorded. "His wife was on horseback with her new-born infant in her arms; another, aged two years, was wrapped in a blanket and slung at her side. One would have said from her air, that nothing had happened to her." Six days later the Dorion baby died and was buried along the trail, another sacrifice to the settling of the West.

On their journey the party separated to try to get food, which was almost unavailable. In the struggles to find food, her husband and the men in their small group were massacred, and she was left with the two small children, a buffalo robe, a knife, and a horse. She loaded the horse, put the children on top, and led the horse through snow in rough country for nine days. She selected a lonely spot in the Blue Mountains for winter camp, killed and dressed the horse, and hung the meat for safety in a tree. Here she and the children spent nearly two months in a shelter she made from pine branches packed with moss and snow. When the meat was almost gone and she knew that she could not stay longer, she set off on foot carrying the children across the mountains, with little to eat for the last week and nothing at all for the last two days. On the fifteenth day she saw smoke in the distance. She left the children wrapped in the buffalo robe and went ahead, scarcely able to crawl. Night came and she had to sleep. At noon next day she dragged herself into the camp of friendly Walla Wallas who rescued the children before nightfall. They lived through the hardships and they and their children have continued to live in the Grand Ronde Valley. Their story was one the old Klickitats often told.

After continued difficulties the Astorians sold out to the Northwest Company, and in 1814 greater efforts were instigated on the Columbia. Most of the men felt "the lure of the West" and continued on with the British. For the next ten years Fort Astoria, now named Fort George, was the principal depot of their westernmost department. It was connected with Fort William by an overland express, and in addition supplies were brought in and its furs exported by sea.

The men continued to have Indian wives and the squaws were usually eager to make the alliance, as it brought them beads, bright cloth, and other things they desired. The men wanted their wives to make a good appearance and the young squaws were eager for bright clothes. The Company frowned on their having children, as that led to more complications, but the

Indians had their secret methods of birth control, if they desired to use them. The Indians treated halfbreed children well. After their trapping days were over, most white men left their Indian wives without remorse, and few Indian women wanted to leave their own people. Many trappers finally settled down in the Willamette Valley, but it was the military men who came later that left their wives behind when they received orders to change posts, because many of the wives were afraid to go to "all those strange people."

The fur traders learned that it took a special type of men to run their boats. These voyageurs, as they were called, or canoemen were recruited in the first place from the French Canadians and later their halfbreed sons. They were light hearted and good natured, sang constantly, and yelled lustily as their boats hit the rough water. They were capable of great endurance. For six months at a stretch in their voyages across the country they rowed or carried loads at the portages from dawn until nightfall, with two twenty minute intervals for breakfast and dinner. Four hours were often their allowance for sleep when it was possible and desirable to go on after dark. At the portages each man took two bales, 160 pounds each, on his back. With the load partly supported by straps across their foreheads, they would trot along for miles. The food of the boatmen was mostly meat. In the West they had no bread or vegetables, but they were allowed eight pounds of meat per day and ten pounds if there was bone in it. It might be buffalo, deer, or horse. In the fall the ration was often two geese or four ducks, and it was sometimes an equivalent amount of fish. In wet weather or on long portages a glass of rum was issued. At Christmas and New Year flour was provided for cakes and puddings, and each received half a pint of rum. They called this the regal or royal privilege. The voyageurs wore capots made of blankets over striped cotton shirts, leather or cotton trousers, moccasins, hats or fur caps, and belts of variegated worsteds from which hung their knives and smoking bags.

There was a lot of portaging in those fur gathering days, when supplies were brought in and furs gathered for shipment by sea. The boats would run in brigades of nine or more. On approaching a post, the boatmen would wear their best clothes, sing their best songs, and play their liveliest tunes on horns and bagpipes. Rowing their fastest, flags flying, they would come in with a grand flourish. The Indians always enjoyed this fanfare and would be on hand to welcome the incoming brigade. The brigades were less apt to be molested because of the number of men, and all this activity passed through the Klickitat settlement on the Columbia. It was the lone traveler who was in most danger.

Ross became a veteran fur hunter after living forty-four years on Indian frontiers, with fifteen of those years on the Columbia. He married an Indian woman and raised a halfbreed family. He came to Astoria in 1812 and worked, later, with the Northwest Company. After the merger with the Hudson's Bay Company, he worked for them at Vancouver.

Ross was often greeted with an Indian's, "Haugh owe yea ah," which was what the Indian understood the white man was saying with his, "How are you all." He also gave us the story of an Indian feast which gives an understanding of Indian customs and what the trader had to face.

"At the feast, the squaws do all the work, and the first thing that the invited guest sees is a train of women going to the banqueting lodge carrying pieces of greasy bark, skins of animals, and old mats. The next thing he sees is a burly savage, who stands at the entrance of the lodge swinging a club to keep the dogs from making a raid on the food.

"The banqueting hall is a roomy wigwam, large enough for the company expected. There is a fire in the center, around which are arranged different kinds of food. When the time arrives, the guests form themselves into a large circle around the whole. Everyone approaches with a grave and solemn step. The stranger is one of them. He squats, with the chiefs on mats laid out for them, and holds between his knees a bark platter which is filled to overflowing with a mixture of Indian foods: bear's grease, dog flesh, berries, Wapato, and other roots.

"Since there is no silverware, nobody needs to worry about which fork to use. Each dives into the mixture with his fingers. If these get too greasy, he wipes them on his hair. Only one knife is present, and that is handed from one to the other. After the feast the dogs are let in to lick the dishes."

Ross Cox was one of the other clerks who left us with stories of their experiences. Because he made nine trips through the Columbia gorge, the Klickitats must have had many opportunities to learn more from him of white man's ways. He lived among the Indian tribes, fought several skirmishes with the Indians, and was lost in the wilderness for fourteen days.

He was a lover of nature, and took trouble to describe plants, animals, and scenery. He was not fond of the Indians but was interested in studying their ways of living. He describes a trip up the river in the following manner. "The day has arrived when the brigade of boats starts up the river. For six weeks, they have been getting ready for it. Here are the voyageurs, happy, husky French Canadians who have come across the continent to work for the Astorians. They have few worries as long as they have a boat to paddle, tobacco to smoke, and occasionally a nip of rum."

The Cascade portage Cox describes as follows. "At the upper portage the Indians assembled in great numbers, but conducted themselves peaceably. They were far more filthy and ugly than the natives around Astoria. The men wore no clothing and the women but little. Their teeth were almost worn away, many had sore eyes, and not a few were blind. The blind ones were treated with much cruelty by the others. When we distributed tobacco, they seemed satisfied and willing for us to go on our way."

In due time they came to the Narrows, which the French Canadians called The Dalles. It is here that for about three miles the Columbia is crowded into a narrow channel not more than seventy yards wide where the waters rush through with frightful force, creating masses of foam and a succession of whirlpools. They had to carry all their goods from the lower to the upper narrows, a distance of about nine miles. It was desperately hard work because of the rocks and took two days under the protection of an armed guard.

Indians, including chiefs, stayed around and watched them at their work, and Cox gave them small gifts in order to try to win their friendship.

Competition in the fur trade grew keener and more ruthless. It is said that the Northwest Company, especially, were plying the Indians with liquor in order to swing deals in furs. In the year 1803 they were reported to have used 21,299 gallons of liquor in this way. As bad as the 50 proof liquor already was, they would dilute it with up to half water, then add red pepper for bite and tobacco for color. If the Indians became unruly from too much of these concoctions, they were given laudanum or opium to quiet them. They became completely demoralized.

To eliminate the rivalry, the Hudson's Bay Company bought out the Northwest Company in 1821, and by 1825 had moved the post up river to a new site, which became known as Fort Vancouver, on the north bank of the Columbia a few miles east of its confluence with the Willamette.

Dr. John McLoughlin was appointed Chief Factor of the new venture. He was a man of patience, just and kind, and strict of conduct for himself and others. His word was law, and he was impressive because he was six feet four inches in height, of more than 200 pounds, with sharp blue eyes and long white hair. Fort Vancouver became so well established that rival traders, including Americans, were effectively barred from doing business. The Fort dwellers raised gardens and crops, introduced cattle and sheep, and conducted their lives with great pomp and circumstance.

No one was allowed to enter the stockade except through the front gates, being formally greeted by a bugle call and passed by the guards. All meals were announced by bugle call, and dinner guests were entertained by the skirling of bagpipes. The men ate in the large dining room at damask covered tables from fine china and polished silver. Some of this same china and silver may be seen at the McLoughlin House in Oregon City, now a museum. The women, the few that came, ate in their rooms or with Mrs. McLoughlin in her sitting room. This formality appealed to the Indians.

It is interesting to find that a band of about twenty Klickitats were invited to make their home at Fort Vancouver and act as the official hunters for the Company dining room. These Indians were selected because they were the best riders and the best marksmen of any of the tribes around. They needed to be good because meat of various kinds was the chief item on the menu, and for eight hundred diners a lot of game and fish were needed, and variety was always demanded. This meant that the hunters had to go some distance to procure fish on the Columbia; ducks and geese from the large island just below Vancouver; deer, elk, and bear from the wooded areas north of the Columbia; and even across the river into the Willamette Valley.

Dr. McLoughlin was married to a halfbreed woman, the widow of Alexander McKay, who had been with MacKenzie on his explorations and later lost his life in the Tonquin massacre on Nootka Sound. She was part Chippewa, had been educated in Canada, and spoke both French and English. She was a good-looking woman of great charm and kindness and was a help to McLoughlin in understanding the natives, as they felt a great trust in her.

George Simpson was the governor of the Northwest Company's Fort Vancouver-based region and as such was both ambitious and efficient. He improved his department's organization and practices of man power. He practised economy to such an extent that he was not well liked by his subordinates. But he developed the Company into something far beyond the needs of the fur trade. The department comprised the whole Pacific Northwest from the Russian settlements in the north to the Spanish in the south, and from the ocean to the Rocky Mountains. Believing the area to the south and west would eventually go to the Americans, he recommended a policy of "trapping out" that region, which meant it would hold less inducement for trappers and settlers to come in. In addition, he wanted a rich return of furs to carry the cost of developing the rest of the department, which he planned to make a permanent occupation.

This meant a policy of conservation of beaver in the rest of the area, and the building of forts and trading posts meant Indian trade instead of buying the furs from roving bands of trappers. He believed that increasing the wants of the Indians not only made a good return for the Company but also had a civilizing effect on the natives.

The site of Vancouver had been chosen to replace Astoria. It was on a bluff overlooking the river, and David Douglas, the botanist, called it "sublimely grand" with its lofty, well-wooded hills, nearby mountains covered with snow, extensive natural meadows, and plains of deep fertile soil. There were stretches of a rich sward of grasses and a profusion of wild flowers. But Simpson's eyes saw the prairie land turned to cultivated fields and pasture for herds of cattle.

While Simpson was governor, it was the Factor or Dr. McLoughlin who became the "hyas tyee" in the eyes of the natives. There was much to do. Dr. McLoughlin was a compassionate man, but he was strict and would punish any infraction of rules. He had a violent temper, and would use his cane, if necessary, to put a point across, but the Indians had respect for him as well as trust.

The Fort was rebuilt in 1828-29 so as to be more convenient to the river for the loading and unloading of furs and supplies. The annual ships brought supplies and the brigades brought the furs down the river. Furs had to be cleaned and baled in readyness for the ship's departure. The expeditions had to be sent off, and the returning brigades welcomed with salutes and cheers. The agricultural work had to be supervised and reports had to be prepared.

With all this hustle and bustle, the Klickitat hunters were kept busy, and as game grew scarcer, they ventured into virgin territory as far as the Umpqua River and learned of attractive sites for new villages.

Things had to be sent out on the overland express, which operated on schedule to carry messages, mail, passengers, and letters to children in school back at Red River, York, and Montreal. The seventy-pound dispatch boxes were carried over portages with their contents of written reports expressing hopes, fears, and loneliness of these early Columbians. At Vancouver there was bustle and excitement, but out in the posts there was no glamour and much hardship. Food was often scarce or impossible to get. The Indians were sometimes sullen and the winters were hard. Those stationed at the outposts were happy to be called in for a trip to Vancouver.

McLoughlin advocated building up lumber trade. A saw mill was built six miles east of Vancouver, which supplied local needs. Another mill was built at Oregon City because of the great number of trees available there. A shipment of lumber was made to the Hawaiian Islands and sold for $100 a thousand board feet. However, the mills eventually had to be shut down because there was no market for the lumber, and trees do not make an industry without a market.

For twenty years the Hudson's Bay Company had been in control. After Astor's unsuccessful attempt, no organized fur companies of American origin tried to cross the Rockies. An American firm of Generals Ashley and Andrew Henry set up rendezvous sites in the mountains, and while their contribution to the trade was not original, it gave a new direction. They abandoned the practice of building trading posts, and instead, they employed trappers who in large and small groups hunted the rivers and streams and brought their accumulated furs to some previously agreed place of meeting. The yearly rendezvous, usually held in July, very soon became a gathering, not only of employees, but of free trappers and Indians as well. At the height of rendezvous in the early 1830's, several thousand Indians and hundreds of white men would assemble and settle accounts. Sometimes as much as two weeks were given over to the lusty carousal, where they drank great quantities of rum and alcohol, fought, and sang. Here the Indians were notoriously cheated by the slick agents. After they had recovered from their spree, they separated for another year of work in lonely and dangerous country.

The fur trappers had to survive both rendezvous and mountain life. Few lived to retire to civilization. The Fur Company supplied the men with goods at a rate to assure themselves a good profit. In 1826 gunpowder sold for $1.50 a pound, scarlet cloth for $6 a yard, beaver traps were $9, sugar $1 a pound, coffee $1.25, flour $1.50, and rum, which greased the wheels of their industry, was $13.50 a gallon. The trappers received $3 a pound for the beaver pelts, and wages were $120 to $600 a year, depending on the competition. The trapper was usually in debt when the accounts were settled.

By this time the demand for fur was declining, because change inevitably comes to any style. The popularity of the beaver hat was on the wane as the silk hat became the favorite in men's headdress. Prime pelts were becoming less common as the numbers of beaver diminished.

The Hudson's Bay Company had done well in its agriculture and cattle raising. It had learned that the Indians were not interested in farming and they were seldom steady, reliable workers. The Company had been both an aid and deterrent to the occupation of the Oregon country by the Americans. To maintain its monopoly, it fought its competitors who might get a foot-hold in the region, and it had resources, men, and capital to carry out reprisals.

By disciplining the natives, by maintaining posts at strategic locations, and by laying out routes of travel, the company lessened the dangers for those adventurers who dared to enter the territory. While the Company discouraged its rivals, it was not ruthless in the treatment of the strangers who came. John McLoughlin made Vancouver an outpost of civilization.

The Indians were becoming used to trading at the post and to this day there are dresses in the Maryhill Museum of Hudson's Bay cloth. The way of life of the Klickitats was changed by all the contacts with fur traders and fur trading activities.

IX

The Coming of Settlers

The long trek through the wilderness by covered wagon.

In the early 1830's, there was much religious interest among the Flathead Indians in Montana, no doubt instilled by the Iroquois who had adopted the Christian faith and had come as proselytizers, some remained and intermarried. Their leader, a zealous teacher of the Catholic faith and inspired by a desire to know more of the white man's Book, gathered a party of Nez Perces and a few Flatheads and set out for St. Louis. Four of the Indians consulted William Clark of the Lewis & Clark expedition, now General Clark an Indian agent, who put them in touch with people of the Catholic faith. The Indians were baptized, but two of them sickened and died. Their burial is recorded in the Cathedral register under the names of Narcisse and Paul.

The two survivors were young men who set out on their homeward journey with George Catlin, ethnologist and painter, as far as the mouth of the Yellowstone. He said they came east "to enquire for the truth of a representation which they said some white man had made amongst them, that his religion was better than theirs and that they would all be lost if they did not embrace it." One of the two remaining Indians died near the mouth of the Yellowstone, and the other is said to have arrived safely among his friends.

"The Christian Advocate," a religious paper, in its March 1, 1853, publication gave a highly imaginative account of the trip to secure religious knowledge, a report which was to have far reaching results. The appeal that had been made to the Catholics for missionaries was answered by the Methodists, who had been roused by the moving story in "The Christian Advocate." This call to work issued by the Methodist Mission Board was answered by a young church elder, Jason Lee and his nephew, David Lee, in 1834. However, the missionaries sent out did not stop with the tribe who wanted to know more of the "White Man's Book of heaven," but went on to Fort Vancouver, where Dr. McLoughlin persuaded them to start their work in the Willamette Valley with the promise of a second mission at The Dalles to take care of the Indians of the interior.

There were already a few white settlers in the valley of the Willamette, mostly around French Prairie, who were men retiring from Fort Vancouver. However, the Indians were few, and things didn't look too promising. The missionaries soon learned that their work would have to be done among the children, so as soon as the mission was built, they started a school of about twenty children. The Indians would bring their sick children to the mission; however, if the young ones died, as sometimes happened, the parents became distrustful and beligerent. Because much of this sickness was due to malnutrition, and because food obviously was needed, the missionaries directed their work toward agriculture. They have been criticized for this in later times. On the other hand, it was natural for them to feel that a strong basis of operation should be established in order to be of help to the Indians, both body and soul, and to ask the Mission Board for more helpers in 1837.

Although there were only eighty-six white Americans in Oregon at that time, they all felt there were opportunities for a great state in Oregon. David Lee went East to plead for reinforcing his mission, and he was successful in securing twenty-one helpers, of which five were ministers. With their families they totaled fifty persons. The mission, when they reached it in 1840, assumed a secular character. Complaints from Oregon to Eastern headquarters brought about a change, and in 1844, Rev. George Gary relieved Lee, who later died on a trip to the East.

To establish the mission at The Dalles, Daniel Lee and H. K. W. Perkins came up the river from the mission at Salem on the Willamette. They stayed overnight at Chief Mark's village, Kle-Miak-Sac, where they camped on Rock Creek and where they gathered the Indians around a camp fire. The next day they were met by Cali-e-wit, a local Indian, who offered to carry their things up to Ka-Klas-Ko, which he told them would be the best place, for it had both grass and water. Ka-Klas-Ko was a mile from the Columbia River, sitting on a hill overlooking the valley toward the east and down toward the entrance of the Columbia Gorge.

By May eleven acres had been planted to corn, potatoes and wheat. The creek flowing through the mission grounds had been diverted for irrigation of the row crops. A rail fence enclosed twenty acres where logs were cut and dragged to the site for a house.

The Wascos, who lived in this area, soon learned that the Sabbath was observed. They became accustomed to attending services, sitting around in the warm sunshine while Cali-e-wit interpreted to suit the Wasco fancy.

A Hudson's Bay trapper lived near the mission and was happy to have neighbors. He would watch out for Mr. Lee while Mr. Perkins went to Salem to get his wife and bring her back with him. After Elvira Perkins came, the squaws were enamored with her and her duties. They watched her knead bread, clean floors, and prepare food. She translated songs and prayers with the help of Cali-e-wit and taught the Indians to sing. She went down the river to have her son born in December at Salem and returned in February. They were all happy to have her back and were intrigued in watching her care for the little white baby. She, in turn, soon had them reciting the Lord's Prayer and singing "Jesus, Lover of My Soul" in their native tongue.

The missionaries kept guard over everything, as the Wascos had many wild parties, often spending a night in a ceremonial dance, even gashing themselves with sharp stones, and whooping and yelling as they danced and "rummed." There were warnings also of hostiles among the Klickitats on the other side of the river. Daniel Lee decided to go down to Vancouver to get guns and ammunition to better protect themselves and he was back in a week with firearms.

During the winter of 1839-40 the Reverend Perkins, Elvira, and Reverend Lee went from village to village telling the Indians to confess their sins and pray for salvation. Many converts had been made during the winter and by April camp meetings were held at Cow-e-laps, a beautiful meadow six miles west of Ka-Klas-Ko. Word was sent out to all the natives, who came with their blankets and camping equipment. Their traveling teepees could be set up quickly. The squaws cut willow poles, sixteen to eighteen feet long, drove them into the ground at a thirty degree angle, and tied them together at the top. Then they unrolled their bundles of grass mats and threw the mats over the poles, leaving a hole at the top for the smoke to escape. The round teepees had one door and the long ones had two doors, one at either end. Sometimes as many as twenty or thirty people lived in one lodge. The village could be set up in a couple of hours, the circle of teepees covering as much as half an acre. The most noticeable feature was the protruding tent poles.

At Cow-e-laps it is estimated that about 1,200 men, women and children gathered, though no actual record was kept by the missionaries, who seemed to think that the Mission Board was interested only in the numbers of those actually baptized. The natives had become accustomed to the routine: at sunrise a trumpet called them to prayer, each rose and knelt in prayer, which was followed by singing. Then they washed their hands and faces and all ate breakfast.

Services were held four and five times a day. The women and children sat on robes and mats on one side of the circle, and the men sat on the other side. Both Daniel Lee and Mr. Perkins were sincere and devoted men, and the lessons were interpreted by Cali-e-wit. They sketched each different Bible story on a strip of paper, making it more realistic to the natives, and this paper was called a ladder.

The missionaries gained courage and would go farther from home to conduct camp meetings, even going to the Klickitat tribe where Owhi lived with his people. Other meetings were held on both sides of the Columbia and up the White Salmon River.

Sally Wahkiacus, the Klickitat woman who lived at the crossroads that later became known as Wahkiacus, used to tell of going to the camp meetings. As she had lived to be more than one hundred years of age in 1930, it is quite possible that her recollections were fairly accurate. She told of the pictures on the "ladder," the good food, and the hymn singing and prayers. She would actually try to sing "Jesus, Lover of My Soul" in her broken voice, with a few words still discernible and the rest misplaced or gone with the passing of the years. It is doubtful that she retained much understanding of the Christian religion, but even at the time of her death she had hazy ideas of a Creator and an afterlife, called "Happy Hunting Ground."

During this time of active mission work, Mt. St. Helens erupted, scattering ashes over the surrounding area as far as Ka-Klas-Ko. Besides a thin layer of ashes, no other damage was reported, and the mountain quieted down after a period of years to become a beautiful snow-clad peak.

The active life of the mission lasted about ten years; how long and how far its influence reached, no one can measure. A story of one instance of its influence is well told by Esther Warren, in her Columbia Gorge story:

"A young Klickitat slave boy who had been captured by a Wasco chief, was taken as a companion to the chief's son, which was a common occurrence among the natives, the slave boy being the same age as the chief's son. The chief had refused to accept any religion and proudly claimed, 'I fear not the power nor care for the vengeance of the white man's God; I will have nothing of it!' The chief's family became ill and all of the family passed away, except this small son, the slave boy's companion. When the small son became ill, too, the chief ran to the mission for medicine, since the medicine men had failed with the other members of the family, he was ready to accept other methods. He ran home to the small boy and poured the medicine down the dying boy's throat, but, alas, he was too late. The son died.

"The grief of a great chief is terrible to see. He sat in silence for four days by the bedside, not speaking a word, knowing he would never see his son again. At last, he gave the command, by gesture, that his son was to be prepared for burial, and the slave was to be buried alive with him.

"The chief's small son was carried to the death house on Memaloose, to a vault made of heavy planks. It was thirty feet long and fifteen feet wide, sodded all over except for the low door at one end, only large enough to carry the corpses through. The other dead were piled on either side and the corpse was laid on the bench and the slave boy, who had been the son's constant companion and playmate, with the same play privileges, was laid beside the dead playmate, face to face, limb to limb, and bound strongly with grass ropes.

"Because he was a brave little fellow, the slave boy did not murmur. The vault was left, the door closed and sealed with dirt and rocks. Indian Johnny heard about the burial of the live boy and informed the Perkins that night. They prayed all night and were at the death house at dawn. They removed the dirt and rocks that sealed the entrance, opened the door and waited a minute to let the stench and vapors escape; then entered as soon as possible. The boy had torn from his master and lay unconscious in a pool of blood. Hurriedly, they carried him outside in the open air where he recovered consciousness. When he did, he screamed hysterically and fought them as he thought his tormentors had returned to torture him. When he recognized Mrs. Perkins, he threw his arms about her neck and kissed her again and again. As native children were taught never to show emotion of joy or sorrow, the slave boy's actions were unusual.

"He was carried to the mission house and nursed back to good health, the wounds made by the thongs, cutting the flesh to the bone, healed in a year and so he had only the scars. Mrs. Perkins adopted him and named him Georgie Waters, for a bishop of the same name. Georgie assisted the missionaries in their camp meetings and became an important part of the missionary compound. Later, after spending some time at Jason Lee Missionary School near Salem, he was sent east with Captain Fremont, where he was educated at Columbia College, New York City."

In 1871 he was made an elder in the church at Moscow, Idaho. He came under the influence of Father James H. Wilbur, the famous Father Wilbur who served as school superintendent from 1864 to 1884 and as Indian Agent for the Yakimas at Fort Simcoe. Georgie Waters, who became known as Reverend Stwire, served a church in Portland and then served as Chief of the Yakima Indian Agency upon the death of his brother in 1912. According to the records, his brother was called White Swan, was listed as a Klickitat, and was the man for whom the town of White Swan was named. Reverend Stwire continued as chief until his death in 1932. Such events had much influence on the Klickitats.

The next missionaries to be sent into the Oregon country were the Reverend Henry Spalding, and his wife, Eliza; Dr. Marcus Whitman and his wife, Narcissa; and Mr. Gray. The women were both brides and much has been written about them. As the first white women to cross the Rockies, they had to undergo much inconvenience and hardship, but they received something close to reverence from the rough and lonely trappers with whom they came in contact.

The Spalding party, left behind in the Powder River Valley to travel more slowly with the livestock, arrived at Fort Walla Walla on September 3. Three days later, on September 6, Mrs. Whitman, Mrs. Spalding and their missionary husbands became Hudson's Bay Company's guests in a bateau for Vancouver, nearly three hundred miles away down the Columbia.

Both women kept diaries, and from these original sources one can get the best understanding of what life was really like. Mrs. Whitman's diaries are quoted:

"September 7. We set sail from Walla Walla yesterday at two o'clock p.m. Our boat is an open one, manned with six oars and the steersman. I enjoy it much, it is a very pleasant change in our manner of traveling. The Columbia is a beautiful river...we sailed until near sunset, landed, and pitched our tents, supped on tea, bread and butter, boiled ham and potatoes, committed ourselves to a kind Providence, then retired to rest. This morn arose before sun rise, embarked and have sailed until nine o'clock and are now landed for breakfast...

"Sept. 8. Came last night to the Chutes, a fall in the river not navigable, where we slept and this morning before breakfast made the portage...

"Sept. 9. We came to The Dalles yesterday just before noon...We made fine progress this morning until nine o'clock when we were met with a heavy wind and obliged to make shore...Have lain still all day for the wind...Intended to have been in Vancouver by tomorrow eve. A party of Indians came to our camp this evening. Every head was flattened. These are the first I have been so near as to be able to examine them. Their eyes have a dull and heavy expression.

"Sept. 10. High winds and not able to move today.

"Sept. 11. Came to the Cascades to breakfast, another important fall in the river where we are obliged to make a portage of a mile. The boat was towed along over the falls by a rope. This is another great place for Salmon fishery. A boatload was ready for Vancouver (as we) arrived, I saw an infant there whose head was in the pressing machine...The child lay on a board between which and its head was a squirrel skin. On its forehead laid a small cushion over which a bandage was drawn tight around, pressing its head against the board. In this postiion it is kept three or four months, or longer, until the head becomes a fashionable shape..."

After being delayed by the heavy winds, they reached Fort Vancouver, where they were welcomed by Dr. and Mrs.

McLoughlin and others. Here, Narcissa stayed until November 2, and was welcomed to stay longer, but she preferred to join her husband at the new mission site and to start in their work.

They were busy days. A sawmill was built. Grain fields and gardens were prepared and some planted. As soon as they had a shelter, they started a school, feeling that they could be of the most help among the young people. Dr. Whitman was primarily a medical missionary, and the Indians seemed to have many ailments which needed his attention, but he gave Christian instruction as soon as he could communicate in jargon. One must remember as well that to establish a mission among these always hungry natives was a tremendous task.

For the most part the Indians were friendly and eager to make small homes and gardens. An exception was Delaware Tom, who was from the east and had been educated at Dartmouth College. He was not well liked by the local Indians but he was able to stir up trouble among them and fill them with ill-will toward the Whitmans.

He set up rivalry between Waiilatpu Indians and those at the Catholic Mission in Umatilla, a mission begun by the Catholics set up at French Prairie in St. Paul, Oregon.

The Whitmans had come in 1836, and eleven years later they were still at the station. Matters had not gone too well. They had lost a two-year-old daughter by drowning. The Indians had been fond of the little golden haired child. One chief had brought two dried rabbit's feet as an amulet at the time of the child's birth, but the tribute had so incensed Narcissa that she slammed the door in the chief's face. To her the gift was a dirty and disgusting symbol of heathenism, while to him it was a protective charm to be hung above the child's cradle.

Then there was this feeling toward all medicine men, who were seen as good only as long as their charms and magic worked. When the remedies failed, they could expect revenge and even death. Dr. Whitman was a medical missionary, and while he treated many scores of Indians successfully, now and then, naturally, there would be a fatality. Ungrateful renegades, such as Delaware Tom and Joe Lewis, had come to them starved and without clothes and had lived at the mission ever since, repaying kindness by stirring up hate and suspicion. The Indians recalled the fateful trick pulled on the Coast Indians at Astoria by Duncan McDougall, when years before he had threatened to pull the cork from the whiskey jug and let out the white man's diseases. The Walla Wallas, Cayuses, Nez Perces, and Klickitats were having ·a bad epidemic of measles, probably brought in by a wagon train. Had Whitman pulled the cork?

It had been a hard life for Narcissa. The Indians seemed to be getting nosier and nosier, even going through her personal things. Often her husband had been gone and left her alone. She had a faithful Indian guard, but in his temporary absence one night, an Indian tried to break into her room. Her guard returned just in time to save her.

The blow fell on November 29, 1847. The Indians attacked when all the whites were busy with their usual tasks. An unusually large number of Indians had gathered and were milling about in the yard, but no thought was given to that as a beef was being butchered and Indians always liked to stand around and watch. At this time there were fifty-nine people living at the mission at Waiilatpu, and thirteen others were at the sawmill twenty miles up Mill Creek. There were seventeen men, thirteen women, and forty-two children. For two days the massacre continued. It is impossible to imagine the horrors of those few days.

The treatment of the captive women by the Indians is a matter of controversy. Spalding's hysterical accounts in his published lectures have been denied. The women were at least subjected to annoyance and in some instances to fear of violence. It is said that some of the young girls were raped and taken as wives. Miss Bewley, who was twenty-two years old, had the most trying experience, as the young Indians wanted her and so did Chief Five Crows, who treated her kindly, but it was impossible for the Indians to understand why the white women did not want Indian husbands, when white men were eager to take Indian wives.

Reverend J. B. A. Brouillet, who had just recently arrived at the Umatilla Catholic Mission, and his interpreter rode into Tilaukait's camp and learned of the massacre. The next morning he hurried to the mission and found a grave had been dug and the bodies were being prepared for burial, using the mission sheets as shrouds. All the bodies were carried to the grave, and with the weeping women and children around, the priest read the burial service. The Indians stood at a distance, painted and armed.

In Brouillet's account we read:

"I found five or six women and over thirty children in a condition, deplorable beyond description. Some had lost their husbands, and others their fathers, whom they had seen massacred before their eyes, and were expecting every moment to share the same fate.

"After the first few words that could be exchanged under the circumstances, I inquired after the victims, and was told that they were yet unburied. Joseph Stanfield...had been spared by the Indians, was engaged in washing the corpses, but being alone he was unable to bury them. I resolved to go and assist him, so as to render to those unfortunate victims the last service in my power to give them.

"What a sight did I behold! Ten bodies lying there, covered with blood and bearing the marks of the most atrocious cruelty, pierced with balls, others more or less gashed by the hatchet. Dr. Whitman had received three gashes on the face."

In all there were fourteen killed. Six escaped, three were released and forty-seven were captives. Hall, who had reported the massacre, escaped and was never seen again.

Sir James Douglas, the successor to Dr. McLoughlin at Fort Vancouver, sent Peter James Ogden with a party of sixteen paddlers and a supply of goods to seek release of the hostages. Ogden was a good choice for negotiations, as he was well known by the Indians as a man to be trusted and respected. He called all the chiefs together for a meeting at Walla Walla and gave them a good tongue lashing in their own language. He showed them that they had been foolish to let the impulsive young men sway their judgments; he denied that the Whitmans had tried to poison them; he reminded them of the good things that had come to them through the mission's help; he warned them if the United States brought war, the whole Cayuse tribe would be wiped out. He advised them to give up the hostages for whom he would pay a ransom to the Indians. Many of the tribe had not been in favor of the massacre and felt regret. The chiefs were quick to accept the offer. The captives were delivered and a ransom of sixty blankets, sixty-three cotton shirts, twelve company muskets, six hundred loads of ammunition, thirty-seven pounds of tobacco, and twelve flints were paid the Indians.

There was some suspicion that the Catholics had stirred up the ill will that brought this massacre to a head, but there was no proof. It was almost ironical that the priest had come there and performed the burial rites for the Whitmans and others. There must have been some rivalry between the Catholics and Protestants, for we find that Father Blanchet wrote a letter on September 28, 1841, from Fort Vancouver to a superior:

"...The Methodists are, first, at Willamette, which is about eight miles from my establishment; second, near the Klaptraps, south of the Columbia River; at Nez Quali on Puget Sound; fourth, at great Dalles, south of Walla Walla; and fifth, at the Willamette Falls...In the midst of so many adversaries we try to keep our ground firmly...

"By the grace of God, our cause has prevailed at Willamette. This spring Mr. Demers withdrew from the Methodists a whole village of savages, situated at the foot of Willamette Falls..."

Within thirty days, the provisional government of Oregon had recruited a regiment of five hundred men at Oregon City, the new city of Portland, and the Willamette Valley. The Hudson's Bay Company advanced supplies to the value of $1,000, and the Methodist Mission advanced credit and supplies to the amount of $3,600. This was enough to start a home-grown war, and they went out to punish the Cayuses, who retreated to the mountains, where they stayed quiet through the 1848 emigration.

The murderers and their friends continued to stay on in the mountains until they had little food and no ammunition. They suffered much and finally gave themselves up. These Indians who gave themselves up as guilty were Tilaukait, Tamahas, Klokamas, Quia-ma-shouskin, and Tsaicklkis. They maintained a proud bearing and showed no feeling of remorse. Though the prisoners must have expected a hard sentence, they seemed to hope that the white man's justice would do something for them, and offered fifty head of horses for a successful defense. This offer, coupled with their behavior and the fact that one of them was known not to have any part in the crime, made people speculate as to their motive in surrendering. When questioned, Tilaukait said, "Did not your missionaries teach us that Christ died to save his people? Thus, we die if we must, to save our people." It seems that after the massacre at Waiilatpu, there had been much disagreement in the tribe as to who was responsible. There was much trouble during their two years of wandering, so Tilaukait explained as these five men gave themselves up. They were hanged at Oregon City June 3, 1850. But here we see one of the injustices done to the Indians: the Cayuse tribe had been forced to find five Cayuses to take the blame, whether they were guilty or not.

This had not been a war of white against red men, but a war to gain government and protection for people who came to settle. Peace had presumably been achieved, but Protestant missionary work was ended east of the Cascades, and settlers were not allowed to take up land until treaties could be concluded with the tribes. The Cayuse tribe was broken, its spirit and prestige gone. Deprived of their leaders, they went to the Umatillas, where other Cayuses lived. In a short time the once arrogant tribe lost both its name and its language, besides dwindling in numbers.

No doubt Dr. McLoughlin had been upset by the Whitman massacre and the Cayuse War that ended with the hanging of the five at Oregon City. It is quite certain these events would not have taken place had he still been in power, but he had resigned from his duties at Vancouver and retired to the Falls of the Willamette, where he settled and hoped to become an American citizen. He suffered many injustices from the people whom he had helped, and it was not until five years after his death in 1857 that restitution was made to his heirs. James Douglas had been appointed factor in his place, but the Indians had not yet learned just how strong a man he could be in their dealings with him. He did not have the control that Dr. McLoughlin had built up.

As has been noted, the missionary effort was not a success, although we have no way of knowing how much physical and spiritual good had been accomplished by these missionaries who sacrificed their health and lives in the effort. The Catholics, who had come in their black robes and more elaborate service made a greater impression on the Indians. It may help one understand the missionary effort when one realizes that the Indians did not believe that men should do manual labor. They had seen Protestant men such as Lee and Whitman and others in the fields and gardens, plowing, sowing, and harvesting, whereas the Catholic priests hired laborers to do the heavy work. To the Indians such work was "squaw work." They felt that a God who made men work was not for them. The missionaries were criticized because they had been so busy in agricultural pursuits instead of teaching and preaching. What should they do? Just starve? Many of those persons who had come with the missionaries gave up the missionary effort and settled down for themselves on the free land that the government was beginning to offer.

X

The First Settler in Klickitat

Their home went up in flames when the Indians attacked.

But now came a white man and his wife looking for free land. In the fall of 1852, Erastus S. Joslyn and his wife, Mary, arrived in Portland from Massachusetts by way of the Isthmus of Panama. The Joslyns took the trip up the Columbia in one of the little steamboats that were in service between portages. With heavy east winds and delay at the portages, it took three weeks to take a look at the country as far as The Dalles. They wintered in Portland, before returning to their chosen spot near what is now called Bingen. When they did return in April, 1853, they found that Indians had undisputed possession of the land. Joslyn dealt fairly with them, calling in the chiefs and paying them for the land with blankets, flour, cloth, and many little things that the Indians had grown to like.

They found some of the Indians were good workers as they had learned that it was to their advantage to help the white folks get settled for they felt that the white folks gave them protection from hostile Indians. The first pre-emption law was passed in 1801 and referred to the lands east of the Mississippi. The Pre-emption Law of 1841, the fifty-first pre-emption act, was applicable to the Oregon country and was written to protect the free trappers, who had lived in the Oregon country for as long as thirty years. This applied to land not yet surveyed, resulting in the claims being irregular and creating a great task for the Surveyor General and his work forces.

New difficulties were brought by the Donation Act of 1850, which invited settlers to take land, whether surveyed or not, and without regard to the extinguishing of Indian titles or the definition of lands guaranteed by treaty to the British. The Hudson's Bay Company was resentful, and the Indians were suspicious. The first settlers got large claims, 320 acres for a single man and 640 acres for a married couple, if married before December 1, 1851. Emigrants who came after December of 1851 were allowed only half the acreage allowed the earlier arrivals.

In February, 1853, an amendment extended the expiration date of the act to 1855, and permitted settlers to patent their claims after two years occupancy and payment of $1.25 an acre. The location chosen by the Joslyns was not settled because the White Salmon area had not yet been opened for claims.

This land was railroad grant land and had not been surveyed, but the Joslyns had the right to file on it under the pre-emption laws which gave them first rights when the land became available.

The Joslyns built a house and a barn, using logs from their own land. They fenced and planted an orchard and garden. A few acres were plowed and planted to grain, corn, and potatoes. Living with the Joslyns was Sammy Ward, who had lost his parents on the trip across the continent and had adopted the Joslyns as his parents. They, having no children and being kind hearted, were happy to help the boy. They continued to enlarge their fields and herds and as the Indians were friendly, things went well. They were isolated, it is true, but the little river steamer called at their shore and provided access to both Vancouver and The Dalles.

Mrs. Joslyn used Indian women for work around the house and found them willing and friendly. The Joslyns being religious people, tried to teach Christian principles by starting a Sunday School. It was well attended and seemed to be appreciated.

A hired man, Mr. Valentine, lived with them also, as there was much work to do. An Indian, Sapot-i-well, and later his wife, worked for them as well. It was they who disclosed the plot of hostile Klickitats and Yakimas to destroy the property and murder the members of the family. The Joslyns heeded Sapot-i-well's warning. Mrs. Joslyn went to the Atwell's across the Columbia, while Mr. Joslyn went to The Dalles to plead with the army there, begging them to consider the problem. General Grant, stationed at Vancouver, and Lt. Sheridan had previously been warned by their Indian scout, Spencer, who was part Klickitat, but it all fell on deaf ears.

When the hostiles learned that the Joslyns had escaped, they planned to take revenge on Sapot-i-well, whose warning had upset the plans.

On May 1, 1856, Valentine, who along with Sammy Ward had not left, went to the pasture to milk a cow. He heard a noise in the willows nearby, but without turning his head to look, he picked up the milking stool, and moved the cow closer to the willows, and continued milking as if nothing had happened. Sapot-i-well's voice came from the willows in a whisper, "White man, leave now, Indians come, kill everybody."

Valentine, after finishing the milking turned the cows and calves together, and called Sammy to join him. They made their way to the river's edge where the willows were thickest and there spent a night of terror hearing the Indians close to them, prowling about. When morning came, they hailed The Dalles boat and were taken across the river to the Coe farm where they found Sapot-i-well and his wife.

From the Oregon side of the Columbia the Joslyns watched the howling Indians set fire to their house, after they had ransacked the buildings, the fruit trees, in full bloom and just coming into bearing age, were chopped down or broken down, their gardens with the green sprouted rows of vegetables were tramped or ripped out, and the cattle and horses were driven off. To see everything they owned wantonly destroyed and to know that the authorities were unconcerned was a hard blow to take. On the other hand, they knew if it had not been for the friendly Indians giving them warning, they would have been tortured and killed. It was a band of renegade Indians that brought this hardship to them which slowed the progress of the Indian problem just that much more.

This incident, perpetrated by a band of renegade Indians, was a serious set-back in white-Indian relations.

XI

Nomadic Life

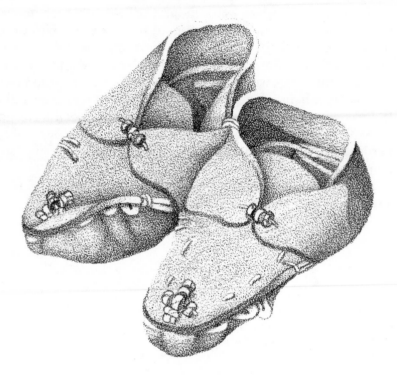

Moccasins, the last thing an Indian wants to relinquish.

One may wonder what all these incidents and tragedies had to do with the Klickitats. But the Klickitats were a nomadic people. While they had been doing the hunting for Fort Vancouver, they had grown fond of the Willamette Valley, where they had often gone for game. They continued to visit that area with their families as game was plentiful, the soil was rich and grew fine gardens, the grazing was good for their horses, and the climate was less severe. Because they liked what they saw, they settled their families in camps while they continued to hunt and rove. Some say the Klickitats conquered the lazy Calapooias and made vassals of them. This is uncertain, although they bragged that they taught the Calapooias to ride and hunt. It is most likely that they just settled amongst them.

Records show that there were Klickitats in the Willamette Valley in the late 1840's. The settlers told of using Klickitats for help in their farming, as they were some of the few Indians who were good workers. There are records of several court cases involving Klickitats, one being a case where the Klickitats claimed that some lumber cut by a settler was theirs, as the trees belonged to them, and the settler avowed the lumber was his because he owned the land. As settlers were beginning to come into the valley, more problems arose for the Indian Agent, Russell Palmer, who ordered the Klickitats back to their former homes so that he might deal only with the Calapooias. The Klickitats left grudgingly, for they felt the land was theirs by right of conquest.

The Klickitats are accused of being a warlike tribe, and it is on record that when the first war broke out with the Rogue Indians, Governor Lane had to raise a volunteer army, and he had a band of Klickitats among them. Under Chief Quatley, they numbered from fifteen to sixty, depending on the source book read. Governor Lane considered them good soldiers.

Again, we hear of them down on the Umpqua, where an adventurous explorer, while looking for gold, told in his diary of getting into trouble with the hostile natives. He knew there was a camp of Klickitats a couple of miles up river, and he told of his efforts to reach them for help. He said that any wayfarer was happy to have the Klickitats come on hunting and fishing trips as they were always friendly to the whites.

Down in what is now Lane County in Oregon, near the east end of a ridge called Klickitat, is a mountain called Klickitat. It is unusual that the name of an Indian tribe, whose home was near Mt. Adams on the Columbia River, should be given to a mountain so far from their home, and yet it is one more evidence to verify the story that the Klickitats traveled far and wide.

In pioneer days there was a trail near Rickreall Creek known as Klicktat Trail, and there was a definite Klickitat camping place near Boyle Lakes, northwest of the present community of Rickreall. J. W. Nesmith, in a letter to *The Oregonian*, of February 7, 1877, says that in September, 1849, he and Governor Lane went from Willamette Valley to the Siletz River over a trail used by the Klickitat Indians who at that time were living in King's Valley.

The Indians were not interested in the politics of the area except where they were directly affected. Their relation with Washington, D.C., came through the services of their Indian agent. The agents were to act as intermediaries between the individual tribes and the President. Many different systems were used in the selection of the agents, resulting in some very fine choices who treated the Indians honestly and humanely, while others turned out to be interested in gaining a fortune and in cheating whenever possible. It was impossible for the Government in Washington, D.C., to have an understanding of the situation when distances were so great.

The big change that came to the country in the Northwest was the passage of the Donation Land Law of 1850, in which the Federal Government gave settlers a free choice of lands from the public domain in the Pacific Northwest. By its own customary practice, the Government did not have title to that land. From colonial times the government had recognized the sovereignty of the Indians over their traditional lands. To acquire title to these lands it made treaties with the Indians, who, in exchange for gifts, annuities, and promises of peace, ceded their rights to the soil.

Washington became a Territory in 1853, with Isaac I. Stevens appointed as its Governor, and was defined as the land lying between the summit of the Rockies and the Pacific Ocean and from the 49th Parallel to the middle of the main channel of the Columbia River until its direction changed at Walla Walla and thence eastwardly on the 46th Parallel. Stevens was an army man, and he was rewarded for his political services to President Pierce with the concurrent offices of Governor of the Territory, Superintendent of Indian Affairs, and leader of the Northern Pacific Railway Survey. The Pacific Railroad Surveys between 1854 and 1861 were well known to the Klickitats because they were made through Klickitat Territory. The Indians had learned to be wary of surveyors and their promises.

Governor Stevens secured the assistance of George B. Mc-Clellan for the duty of exploring the Cascade Mountains. Mc-Clellan left St. Paul in May with 243 men, including eleven army officers and a staff of artists and scientists, later being joined by a group of fifty-two men under Lieutenant Rufus Saxton, who came from The Dalles. Saxton was stopped by each tribe as he traveled east, with a challenge as to his bringing an armed force across their lands. He satisfied them all and served as advance agent for the governor.

Authority to negotiate with the Indians was granted under the Indian Treaty Act of 1850. Commissioners were appointed to make treaties with the western Indians and remove them to unsettled areas east of the Cascades. The Commissioners found the Indians willing to cede their lands but refusing to move to different territory. When one considers the differences in environment—rainy wooded areas and dry barren plains—one can see the wisdom on the part of the Indians. The Commissioners eventually departed from their instructions and agreed that the Indians should retain a portion of their old lands while ceding the remainder. Between 1851 and 1853 treaties were negotiated between some Willamette Valley tribes as well as some coastal bands.

It is worth noting that the Indians in the western part of the territory were on the whole willing to make the concessions in exchange for annuities, provided they did not have to move, whereas those in the interior had a different attitude toward their land and did not want to part with any of it. The Yakimas and their neighboring tribes had an exclusive sense of ownership. They required outsiders to get permission to cross their lands and even posted guards to forbid access. The failure of the Senate to ratify Indian treaties left the matter of land titles wide open. Settlers did not wait, they just came.

Governor Stevens began his work of peacemaker with the Pieganns and the Blackfeet before leaving Fort Benton. Stevens said in his report that he was conscious of an oversight on the part of the whites, himself included, in their formal negotiations with the natives. "On all solemn occasions when I met the Indians on my route, they were arrayed with utmost care. My duties in this field did not allow the same attention on my part, and the Indians sometimes complained of this, saying, 'We dress up to receive you, and why do you not wear the dress of a chief?' This was a detail which the experienced officials of the British Fur Companies had never overlooked. The Indians attended their councils with ceremony and formality." They expected the same courtesy.

Settlers had been coming in great numbers in the 1840's, going down through the Columbia gorge, passing the Klickitats only to portage or to trade. A few had stopped at The Dalles or on the south side down river toward the Cascades, a few finding work in the sawmills or as carpenters. The land on the north side of the river had not been opened for settlement, as it had been given to the railroads as an inducement to build. The tract was forty miles wide and limited to every other section.

The Indians lived much as usual, dug their camas, camped at the base of the mountain while picking huckleberries, gathered grass for their baskets, and fished at their usual spots. But they saw the advantages that the whites possessed as they traveled through.

XII

The Klickitats

Pa-Toe (Mt. Adams), home of the Indian gods.

Everyone felt that trouble was brewing in the Northwest. The Indians were sullen as the coming of settlers continued to bring new problems. Congress had authorized Governor Stevens, acting as an Indian Agent, and Joel Palmer, the agent in the Oregon area, to make treaties, and had appropriated funds for the purpose. In the winter of 1854, Stevens sent an agent, James Doty, among the tribes to invite them to a council meeting in May in order to explain the Government's proposals.

On his railroad survey Captain George McClellan came through the Klickitat area in 1853. Because of high water on the

Columbia he was investigating mountain passes and higher ground. His reports show he came in by way of Twin Buttes, Peterson Prairie, Trout Lake, Glenwood, and Blockhouse, all familiar places to modern huckleberry pickers. McClellan was censured for the way he did his job, but we do have a report from Lt. George Gibbs that he sent to his superior, which gives an insight into the character of the Klickitats.

Report of Lt. George Gibbs sent to Captain McClellan in 1854:

"The Klickitats and Yakimas will remain in the Washington Superintendency. The former inhabit, properly, the valleys lying between Mt. St. Helens and Adams but they spread over districts belonging to other tribes, a band of them is now located as far as the Umpqua. Their nomadic habits render a census very difficult, though their number is not large. Dr. Dart stated them at 492, since when, there has certainly been a decrease. The head chief of the Klickitats is a very old man named Tow-e-loks. He evidently possesses but little influence, his people paying more respect to his wealthier neighbors: Kamiakin, Skloom, and other chiefs of the Yakimas.

"The Klickitats and the Yakimas, in all essential peculiarities of character are identical and their intercourse is constant, but the former, though a mountain tribe are more unsettled in their habits than their brethren.

"This fact is probably due, in the first place, to their having been driven from their homes, many years ago by the Cayuses, with whom they were at war. They thus became acquainted with other parts of the country as well as the advantages derived from trade. It was not until about the 1830's that they crossed the Columbia, when they overran the Willamette Valley, attracted by game with which it abounded, and which they destroyed in defiance of the weak and indolent Callapooyas.

"They manifest a peculiar aptitude for trading, and have become to the neighboring tribes what the Yankees were to the Western States, the traveling retailers of notions, purchasing and selling white feathers, beads, cloth, and other articles prized by the Indians and exchanging them for horses which in turn they sell in the settlements. Their country supplies them with abundant food. The lower praries afford kouse, kamaas, and other roots; and the mountains a great variety of berries.

"Of game there is very little left.

"Very few attempt any cultivation of the soil, although their lower valleys would admit of it. We were informed that the next season many of them intend to build houses and plant potatoes. Their usual residence during the summer is around Chequese, one of the most elevated spots on the trail from Fort Vancouver, across the Cascades, where we met them at the beginning of August. They were at this time feasting on strawberries and the mountain whortleberry, which cover the hills around, though during the night the ice formed on the ponds to the thickness of half an inch. Toward the end of the month they descend to the Yahkoutl, Chalache, and Takh Praries, where they are met by the Yakimas, who assemble with them, for the purpose of gathering a later specie of berry, and for horseracing. The racing season is the grand annual occasion of all these tribes. A herd of proved reputation is a source of wealth or of ruin to its owner. On it, he stakes his whole stud, his household goods, clothes, and finally his wives; and a single bet doubles his fortunes, or sends him forth an impoverished adventurer. The interest is not confined to the individual directly concerned; the tribe shares it with him, and the pile of goods, of motley description, apportioned according to their ideas of value, is put up by either party, to be divided among the baskets of the winners. The Klickitats, themselves, are not as rich in horses as those living on the plains. Their country generally affording but little pasturage and the deep snows compelling them to winter their stock at a distance from their usual abodes. The horse is to them what the canoe is to the Indians of the river and coast. They ride with skill, reckless of all obstacles, and with no mercy to their beasts, the right hand swinging the whip with every bound. Some of the horses are of fine form and action, but they have generally been injured by too early use, and sore backs are universal.

"Indiscriminate breeding has greatly deteriorated what once must have been good stock, and the prevalence of white and gray in their colors is a great objection. Wall eyes and white noses and hooves are more than common among them. They are almost always vicious or lazy, and usually combine both qualities. In their capacity for continued endurance, they are over-rated. A good American horse is much superior to them in this, as in speed; but they are hardy and capable of shifting with but little food. Nothing is known of their first introduction. They were abundant when the country was first discovererd. It is probably that the Shoshones or Snakes, a branch of the Co-manchees, first introduced them from the north, and the breed has since been crossed by others from Canada, and the best being those belonging to the Cayuses and Nez Perce. The de-mand for horses, consequent upon the settlement of the coun-try, has rendered the tribes possessing them as really wealthy.

"Their price is from 40 to 100 dollars, but they have some that they will not dispose of at a much higher price. A few of the chiefs have great numbers, and one, it is said, has offered 400 horses, a by no means contemptible dowry, to any responsible white man who will marry his daughter.

"The Indians ride with a hair rope knotted around the under jaw of the horse for a bridle. The men use a stuffed pad with wooden stirrups. The women sit astride, in a saddle made with a high pommel and cantle, and in traveling carry their infants either dangling by the cradle strap to the former, or slung in a blanket from their shoulders, while those of a little larger size sit perched on the pack animals, or hold on as best they can.

"The horses are trained to stand for hours with merely a lariat rope thrown loosely around their necks and trailing to the ground. With the whites they are as shy as American horses or mules are with Indians; but they suffer from the squaws and children with perfect contentment, and hang around the huts like dogs. When camping near them, we found them to be an intolerable nuisance, from their incessant neighing and whinny-ing during the night. Whenever mosquitoes were abundant, they posted themselves in the smoke of the camp fires. It is the business of the squaws, while traveling, to pack the animals, the men contenting themselves with catching them and bringing them up; and they pile on the most heterogeneous assortment of luggage with a skill that would immortalize a professional packer. In breaking horses the Indians usually blind fold them before mounting, often lying down their ears in addition. A strap cord is then passed around the animal, loose enough to admit the knees of the rider. Much time is spent in soothing and quieting the beast, as the Indian has plenty of it on his hands. When everything is ready, he vaults to his back, always from the off side, slips his knees under the girth and tightens it, withdraws the muffle, and sits prepared for a series of stiff legged plunges, ending in a charge. The quick straightening of the leg releases the knee and he is prepared for the emergency.

"In describing the household goods of the Indian, his dogs are not forgotten. They vary in form with different tribes, but always preserve the same general character. Quarrelsome and cowardly, inveterate thieves, suspicious and inquisitive, they are constantly engaged in fights among themselves or prowling among the lodges for food. The approach of a stranger is heralded with short, sharp yelps, succeeded by a general scamper. They all bear the same mysterious resemblance to the coyote — the sharp muzzle and stiffly curling tail. Not withstanding their worthlessness, they seem to have a strong attachment to their owners, and an Indian camp would be a novelty without them.

"Very few characteristic features remain among these people. Their long intercourse with the Hudson's Bay Company and of late years with the Americans, has obliterated what peculiarities they may have had, nor is there any essential difference in their habits or manners from those Indians adjoining them. They use for the most part the arms and utensils of the whites, and the gun has superseded the bow and arrow. The pails and blankets constructed from the bark of cedars, the saddles, and fishing apparatus are their principle articles of domestic manufacture and of such things it is almost as common to find the imported substitutes.

"In regard to moral character, they are much superior to the lower river Indians; not that perfect virtue is by any means to be expected, but they are more strict of their women, particularly the married ones, and they are far less thievish.

"Their mode of disposing of their dead, like that of their kindred tribes, is in the ground, but without any attempts of coffins, the body being wrapped in clothing. Just before our arrival in Chequess, a man had died of small pox, and those who had buried him were purifying themselves. During the three days occupied in this they absented themselves from camp, alternately using the sweat house and plunging into the cold river.

"The house, which was a small oval shape affair, was heated by stones. The mourning is performed by women who live apart for a few days and afterward bathe and purify themselves. They have the common objection to mentioning the name of the dead as well as their own. The practice of medicine as elsewhere, consists of incantations, and is attended with the usual hazards. The life of the practitioner answering for the want of success. Besides these mummeries, however, they use certain plants as medicines, among which are both emetics and cathartics. The patriarchial institutions of slavery and polygamy are yet retained among them; the number of wives being limited only by the wealth of the husband, for with them it is the women that are sold.

"A curious custom exists exhibiting their savage ideas of equity as opposed to the common maxim of 'caveat emptor.' If a wife dies within a short period after marriage, the bereaved husband may reclaim the 'bride prize' from the father, so also it is with slaves and horses.

"No systematic attempt has, it is believed, been made to convert the Klickitat to Christianity, although many individuals came in contact with the missionaries and the Joslyns at White Salmon."

A few Klickitats had had instruction at the Jason Lee Mission at Salem and at The Dalles. They attended revival meetings where they enjoyed the sociability of these get-togethers. They learned hymns and Bible passages. Some were baptized and partook of Holy Communion. They believed in an afterlife, but it is doubtful if any of them had a real understanding of Christianity. They expected to be rewarded in goods or food for attending services.

XIII

Boundaries

Kamiakin, a chief of the Klickitats.
Drawing by Gustavus Sohon, from the Washington State Historical Society Library.

In the winter of 1854 an Indian agent had visited all the tribes in the Columbia area, telling them that a council would be held in Walla Walla in May to explain that the Great White Father in Washington wanted to buy their land and open up the area for the settlement of the white people, who would be coming from the east. Nothing could have been more disturbing to the Indians. Word went out to all the tribes that if they refused to sell part of their land, soldiers would be sent to drive them out. If they refused to meet, soldiers would be sent in and the Indians would be wiped off the earth.

When Owhi told Kamiakin about this threat, he replied, "At last, we are faced with those awful people, the coming of whom was foretold by the old medicine man, Wa-tum-nah, long ago. Peu-peu-mox-mox, who has been in California, says that the Indians are dying off. I have traveled through the Willamette Valley since its settlement by the Whites and found only a small number left of the powerful Multnomahs and Cal-apoo-yahs. So, it will be with us, if we allow the whites in our country. Heretofore, we have allowed them to travel through our land unmolested, and we refused to help the Cayuses make war against them, for we wanted to live in peace and be left alone, but we have been both mistaken and deceived. Now, when palefaced stranger, Governor Stevens, from a distant land, sends to us such words as you have brought me, I am for war. If they take our lands, they will be marked with our blood."

After asking Owhi to arrange for a meeting in two weeks with other leaders, Kamiakin rode to the Catholic mission on the Ahtanum to tell Father Pandozy of the message sent by Owhi. The priest replied, "It is as I feared. The whites will take your country as they have taken other countries from the Indians. I come from the land of the whites far to the east, where the people are thicker than the grass on the hills. While there are only few here now, others will come each new year, until your country will be over run with them; your land will be taken and your people driven from their homes. It has been so with other tribes: it will be so with you. You may fight and delay for a time this invasion, but you cannot avert it. I have lived many summers with you. I cannot advise or help you. I wish I could."

Anyone who has been forced through property condemnation knows the bitterness that entered Kamiakin's heart. With his brother, Skloom, he went to the home of Peu-peu-mox-mox, where they were joined by the Nez Perce chief. Kamiakin told of the message that Owhi had brought from Governor Stevens and laid out plans for a confederacy of all the tribes from British Columbia to the southern boundary of Oregon, for the purpose of resisting, if it became necessary to stop the occupancy of the land by whites. Both of the influential chiefs gave their approval. It was agreed to hold a council in a month, and Governor

Stevens was not told of the plan. All were urged to select able men to attend and to keep this in deepest secrecy.

This council, which met at Grande Ronde in eastern Oregon, was the most important gathering of Indians that had ever been held in the Northwest. It met for five days, and speakers were heard from nearly every tribe. Only Hal-halt-los-set, (Lawyer) of the Nez Perce, Sticas from the Cayuses, and Garry from the Spokanes were in favor of making a treaty with Stevens and selling their lands. All of the interested tribes, except Lawyer and Sticas, met to mark previously undefined boundaries between tribal territories so that at council meetings the chiefs would know what lands they represented, in preparation for establishing reservations for their people.

Boundaries arranged for the Yakimas, Klickitats, Wishrams and Sokulks were the territory extending from the Cascade Falls of the Columbia, north along the summit of the Cascade Range to the head of the Cle-el-lum east to Mt. Stewart and the ridge of the We-nat-sha Mountains, north of the Kittitas Valley, to the Columbia River and across to Moses Lake, thence south to White Bluffs, crossing to the west side and on down to the point of beginning, including all the Yakima, Klickitat and Kittitas Valleys.

The spirit of war was thoroughly aroused. Kamiakin went from tribe to tribe urging them to take a definite stand. Reviewing his memories of the wrongs the Indians suffered, he said, "We wish to be left alone in a land of our forefathers, whose bones lie in the sand hills and along the trails, but a palefaced stranger has come from a distant land and sends words to us that we must give up our country, because he wants it for the white man. Where can we go? Only a single mountain separates us from the big salt water of the setting sun. Our fathers, from the hunting grounds of the other world, are looking down on us today. Let us not make them ashamed. My people, the Great Spirit has his eyes on us. He will be angry if, like cowardly dogs, we give our land to the whites. Better to die like brave war heroes on the battlefield, than to live among our vanquishers despised. Our young men and women would speedily become debauched by their firewater and we should perish as a race."

In the spring Doty arrived telling that the Stevens Council would be held in May at a spot near where Walla Walla now stands. It was quite centrally located with a big enough stretch of plain to accommodate the Indians who always brought their families to camp with them on such occasions, and with enough grass to graze their herds of horses.

XIV

The Walla Walla Treaty

The carved peace-pipe used for the smoking ceremony.

In May came the day for the Walla Walla meeting with Governor Stevens and General Joel Palmer. The Indians were in bad humor, and any mention of Kamiakin tells of the sneer on his face. The Nez Perces were the first to arrive, coming twenty-five hundred strong with men, women, and children, circling Stevens' camp at a gallop, their hoof beats on the hard ground sounding like a flurry of drums. Ten days later the Cayuses arrived, three hundred in all. As each tribe entered the council grounds, they rushed in with yells and whoops, characteristic of their mode of warfare. They would circle the field with their feats of horsemanship, seldom equalled, then go into camp some distance away.

Of the Yakimas, fourteen tribes were represented. They were: Yakima, Palouse, Pisquoise, Wenatshapam, Sjyiks, Ochechotes, Kamiltpah, Klickitat, Klinquit, Kowwassayes, Liaywas, Skinpah, Wishram, and Seapcat as listed on the Treaty Monument at Toppenish. These were confederated tribes and bands of Indians, "Occupying lands hereinafter bounded and described lying in Washington territory, who for the purposes of this Treaty are to be considered as one nation, under the name 'Yakima,' with Kamiakin as its head chief, on behalf and acting for said tribes and bands, and being duly authorized thereto by them."

Kamiakin had been asked by Stevens to represent the fourteen tribes. Each tribe had a number of headmen that the whites called "Chief" as a complimentary title, somewhat as we think of a committee chairman, as head of the hunt, head of the trek for berries, or head of a battle. Chief Kamiakin was such a man and was named as head of the Treaty negotiations. Although he lived in the Yakima area, he was actually a member of the Palouse tribe, for his father was Si-Yi, a Palouse, who lived near Starbuck close to the Nez Perce country, and his mother was Kah-Mash-Ni, a Yakima.

He was a typical North American Indian, the strongest personality of his time in that region. The dominating characteristic of Kamiakin was love for his people and native land, and his desire for the peaceful possession of it. It is said that he never hurt a woman or child, red or white.

A self-made man, he rose to the highest place through his ability as an organizer and leader, not through warlike tendencies, for by nature he was peaceful. Kamiakin was tall, over six feet in height, of superb stature and proportions, sinewy and active.

Theodore Winthrop, the Yale-educated traveler, wrote in his book, *Canoe and Saddle*, "He was a tall man, very dark with a massive square face and a grave reflective look, without the senatorial coxcombry of Owhi, his manner was strikingly distinguished, quiet and dignified. He greeted the priests as a kaiser might a delegate. To me, as their friend, he gave his hand with a gentlemanly word of welcome."

He was held in great esteem as a counselor, and all the tribes called on him to settle disputes. When the Cayuse consulted him after the Whitman massacre, he condemned the act and refused to join with them against the Oregon Volunteers. When Peu-peu-mox-mox consulted with him and Chief Ellis of the Nez Perce about a war of revenge on the settlers for the killing of Peu-peu-mox-mox's son, Elija Hedding, by a white man in California, both advised against it.

Kamiakin's convincing power as an orator and his wide acquaintance throughout the northwest, along with a keen insight into the affairs of different tribes, made him a natural leader. As a youth, he often joined the Nez Perce in buffalo hunts and in their skirmishes with other nations. The fact that his mother came from royalty gave him some standing in the tribe, it was his natural endowments gave him his best claim to leadership.

He married Sal-kow, a daughter of Te-i-as, who was the daughter of his uncle. A few years later he married the daughter of Chief Tennak of the Klickitats and eventually another daughter of Tennak, and when there was trouble at White Salmon, two more daughters came to live with him.

To get the Council underway at Walla Walla many preparations were needed. Interpreters and record keepers were found. An arbor was built for shade and convenience, and the Indians were invited to gather. About a thousand of them assembled, sat on the ground in a semi-circle with the men in front and the women and children toward the rear. After half an hour of smoking, a ceremony that must precede all Indian business, Governor Stevens and General Palmer made long speeches setting forth the plans for the reservations. All the speeches were interpreted and reinterpreted until they were understood by all the Indians. It was soon evident that there were two factions, one a large group under Lawyer, of the Nez Perce, who favored the whites, and the other faction of the Nez Perce and all the other tribes who were against the treaty. With skill, patience, and threats, the two agents, with the powerful assistance of

Lawyer, brought the Indians to a point of agreement, when there occurred one of those dramatic events of history that still stir the imagination.

Suddenly, there was a commotion. Into the midst of the assembly burst the old Chief Looking Glass, second only to Lawyer in influence among the Nez Perce. He and his men had made a desperate ride of three hundred miles in seven days, following a buffalo hunt and raid against the Blackfeet, and even now there dangled from his belt the scalps of several Blackfeet. In Hazard Stevens' *Life of Governor Stevens*, he quotes Looking Glass as saying, "My people, what have you done? When I was gone you sold my country. I have come home and there is not left me a place on which to pitch my lodges. I will talk with you." And thus the work of the Council was nearly undone.

At this time Lawyer went to Stevens with information of a plot to attack him and his camp, and the suggestion that Lawyer move his lodge and family into their midst, as a sign to the plotting Indians that he and his Nez Perces were against any scheme of exterminating the whites.

Stevens said later that he was sure the plot against him and his party was thwarted by this action. A. J. Splawn says in his book on Kamiakin that he lived for fifty years among the Yakimas and talked with many of the old men who had been present at the Council Meeting, some of them men important in their own tribes, and all claimed that there was no foundation of truth to Lawyer's story. They felt that he was trying to advance his own cause in trying to get a better deal for the Nez Perce and that there was no truth in the tale. At any rate he gained the cause he sought. It appears the Indians were no different from the whites in their jealousies and ambitions.

Lawyer was cunning and ambitious. With his education he was aware of the strength and power of the whites and recognized that they had the advantage in war because of guns and ammunition, and in numbers. He knew the inevitable result would be defeat and humiliation for the Indians. By showing friendship to the whites, he thought he could gain advantages for his tribe and recognition for himself. While historians give him much credit for being wise, his Indian neighbors felt at the time that he was a traitor to their cause. However, his descendants, today, look back at him with pride and feel that the Indian problem of the present would be less had they listened more to his advice.

Kamiakin had not yet spoken, and there seems to be some difference of opinion as to whether he did or not, but it is reported that he made the following remark in answer to their urging:

"What have I to say? I have something different to say. It is the young men who have spoken. I have been afraid of the white men. Your chiefs are good; perhaps they have spoken straight that your children will do what is right. Let them do as you have promised. That is all I have to say."

Stevens announced a time for adjournment of the council. On that day, June 11, 1855, Lawyer was asked to be the first to sign the treaty. He was followed by Looking Glass and all the other chiefs, but Kamiakin claimed he did not do so, but there is a mark behind his name. He said he signed only to show good will. Did they or not realize how binding those little crosses behind their names really were? But they knew some sort of treaty was inevitable.

The Yakimas were offered a tract of land of 16,920 square miles, or almost an area of 10,828,800 acres, with annuities of goods to the amount of $140,000, these annuities to last for twenty years, the head chief would receive $500 a year. Many other things were promised, such as schools, roads, houses, machinery, and help in learning how to farm. This was for all the fourteen tribes that were to make up the Yakima Federation. They were to be forced, irrespective of their wishes, to live within an area too small for their sustenance, and to completely change their life style.

Kamiakin had complained of being tired of so much talking. Perhaps the complaint was justifiable as the official proceedings of the Council in the National Archives runs to 30,000 words with many additional notes, so it is small wonder he was tired of "hearing." But they had entertained themselves as well, for they indulged in horse racing, foot racing, stick and bone games, gambling, drumming and dancing. There had been an estimated five to six thousand camped on the Treaty grounds.

Kamiakin stayed while the goods and presents were being distributed for the Yakimas, and Kamiakin, although he would not take any goods for himself, superintended the division. At that time, he did not wish to receive anything, but when the Treaty was signed by the President, if he lived on the Reservation would accept his share. He desired a small piece of land at the place Wenatshapan, where the Indians took fish, and he wanted to go home to tend his garden. They had promised to let people go through their area unmolested.

The Treaty was not effective until signed by the President and this did not come about until April 18, 1859. One wonders why it took so long to get action on so important a matter. Even after the Treaty was signed, funds for fulfilling the agreements were slow in being appropriated. It just added to the Indian mistrust.

The greatest misfortune was that on the one hand the Indians had been promised that the Treaty was not valid until signed, yet on the other hand the lands were at once declared open for settlement before the Indian titles were liquidated. Joel Palmer, the Oregon Indian agent, ran an ad in the *Umpqua Oregon Gazette* on July 26, 1855, making the announcement that the land was open for settlement. James Nesmith, the Superintendent for Indian Affairs in Salem, Oregon, gave out the same information, and even Governor Stevens, who had made the promise, put the same notice in the *Puget Sound Courier* for July 12, 1855. This made the Indians lose yet more faith in the words of the white man.

Governor Stevens reported that the Council had ended in a most satisfactory manner. The Governor, in contrast to Kamiakin, was a small statured man with the egotistical drive common among less favored men, and he was determined to get treaties signed and move on to the next tribe.

In contrast with the signing of the treaty, the Indians felt they were giving up their birthright, land, which the Creator had made especially for them. Their speeches voiced their dissatisfaction and they wanted more time to negotiate in their usual way, making decisions slowly and with much palaver. They wanted to take things back to their home folks for decisions. However, after threats and promises, Stevens, Palmer, and Lawyer got the Indians to reluctantly agree to set aside three reservations, and later a fourth was added. Furthermore, they should not have been threatened with extinction if they refused to comply.

Kamiakin, Skloom, and Owhi crosses appear on the document, but they all claimed they did not give away their land and that they merely made a little mark to show "friendship only."

Did they not understand, or were they later afraid to admit what they had done? The Klickitats accused Kamiakin of selling out their homes. In later years the Klickitats grieved over loss of identity. Perhaps that could have been prevented had they gone to the Council, as invited, and shown their concern over a paragraph in the Treaty which reads, "Confederated tribes and bands of Indians occupying hereinafter bounded and described land, and living in Washington teritory, who for the purposes of the treaty, are to be considered as one nation, under the name of 'Yakima,' with Kamiakin as head chief, on behalf of and acting for said tribes and bands, and being duly authorized by them." Klickitat had been a well known name, but this was one step in the loss of that remembrance.

XV

Hatred Aroused

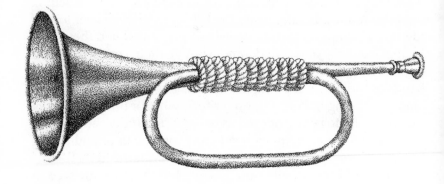

The Indians found out that a bugle call meant "look out."

The immediate result of the treaty making at the Walla Walla Council was to increase the hatred that had been aroused by McClellan's railroad survey. Before 1850 people had passed through the Indian country unmolested. In *Canoe and Saddle*, by Theodore Winthrop, he tells of the tour of adventure riding across the country with a young Klickitat Indian as guide, whom he describes as "reluctant and frowsy." He was able to make this trip without hostile encounter and found several Klickitat Indian families far up in the mountains. He describes the trip with humor, despite the rough terrain and constant food shortage.

He was never fond of the Indians but liked them even less after this journey.

With the discovery of gold in the Colville country, many more travelers wanted to cross the Indian lands. So many, in fact, that it became no longer safe for white men, especially alone, to travel across Indian territory. Rumors reached the settlers that the Yakimas had become hostile to the white man. There were many reports of killings, some verified and some unrecorded.

A. J. Bolon, sub-agent at The Dalles, was disturbed over the news of these killings, and as he was going to Spokane to meet with Governor Stevens, he decided to turn aside and go to see Kamiakin and learn the truth of these atrocities. He went alone in order to show the Indians that he was their friend. He stopped at the lodge of Show-away or Ice, a brother of Kamiakin, who was a good friend and who persuaded him to turn back, which Bolon did. On this return journey he met up with a group of Indians who were on the way to The Dalles to bargain for dried salmon. They camped together and Bolon was treacherously killed, as was his horse, and all burned. Ice, when he heard that his own son was the cause of his friend's death, cried bitter tears. Qualchan was suspected for many years, until an old Indian who had been present at the murder, confessed to Professor Lucullus McWhorter, much interested in Indian history, about the crime he had been afraid to tell so far, for fear of being punished.

After this event a military force was sent in to fight against the Indians, and war would become general. Several companies of volunteers were raised, who furnished their own mounts and rag-tag clothing.

One of the outstanding battles was at Union Gap, for here were gathered many noted chiefs, including Kamiakin, Skloom, Ice, Owhi, and Qualchan of the Yakimas; Moses of the Ke-wah-chins; and Lot of the Spokanes. Most conspicuous on the other side was a young lieutenant, Phil Sheridan, who became a general in the Civil War but who was seeing in the Indian War his first military service. In this battle of Union Gap, the Indians met for the first time the bugle and the howitzer. They were not long left in doubt about the meaning of the bugle, and soon learned of the howitzer when the stone breastwork was scattered in all directions, making the Indians escape into the brush.

Allegiance to the Confederacy that had met at Grande Ronde brought trouble on the Rogue in the south and at Nisqually in the north. The massacres in the Rogue country in the 1850's came as a surprise to the settlers and travelers in that area, because they thought their local Indians were friendly. The signal fires lit on the mountain tops in the Yakima country were what set off their uprisings.

Soldiers and volunteers had retired from the Yakima country when snow and cold put a stop to their activities, and many of the Indians had returned to their homes, when in the middle of January, 1856, a worn and weary Indian arrived at Owhi's lodge, after crossing the Cascade Mountains on snowshoes. He brought word from Chief Leschi of Seattle, asking for help. Leschi was a close relative of the Yakima chiefs, Qualchan being his cousin. Qualchan went westward over the mountains with about one hundred warriors. Leschi insisted on using his own plan of attack, which was unsuccessful, and the Yakimas returned home. At a council meeting they expressed the opinion that further fighting would be useless. "Today's fight has convinced us that you cannot cope with the whites," and advised Leschi and his people to move to the Yakima Valley.

It was decided to act upon this advice, and the retreat began at once. These people had made their brave fight, their last stand for their homes against circumstances too strong for them. In that dreadful retreat over the snowy mountains, with but little food, many old men and women and children perished by the wayside and were buried in the snow. The wails of the women and the crying of the children touched even the stony heart of Qualchan, and he made the following promise:

"The suffering of these people, caused by the whites, has determined me never to surrender or quit fighting them as long as I live." He kept his word.

PHOTOGRAPHS

*The gorge of the Klickitat River, where the Indians
fished for salmon.*

The city of Lyle, Washington.

Celilo Falls, on the Columbia River.

In testimony whereof, the said Isaac I. Stevens Governor and Superintendent of Indian Affairs for the Territory of Washington and the undersigned Head Chief, Chiefs, Head men and Delegates of the aforesaid confederated Tribes and Bands of Indians have hereunto set their hands and Seals at the place, and on the day and year herein before written.

Signed and Sealed in Presence of

James Doty, Secty Treaties

Isaac I. Stevens [S.S.]
Gov. & Supt.

Kamaiakun X [S.S.]

M. Cls. Pandosy O.M.I.

Skloom + [S.S.]

W. C. McKay

Owhi X [S.S.]

W. H. Tappan
Sub Ind. Agent W.T.

Te-cole-kun X [S.S.]

C. Chirouse O.M.I.

Patrick McKenzie
Interpreter

La Hoom X [S.S.]

A. P. Pambrun
Interpreter

Me-ni-nock X [S.S.]

Joel Palmer
Supt Ind Affairs O.T.

Elit Palmer X [S.S.]

Wish-och-kmpits X [S.S.]

Koo-lat-toose X [S.S.]

Shewah-cote X [S.S.]

Tuck-quille X [S.S.]

W. D. Bigelow
A. P. Pambrun
Interpreter

Sla-loo-as x [S.S.]
Seha-noo-à x [S.S.]
Sla-kish x [S.S.]

Names of the Walla Walla Treaty signers, their "X" marks and names of witnesses as they appear on the original Treaty now in the National Archives.

Skookum Wallahee in Washington, D.C.
(Left circle) Skookum, chief of the Klickitats; (Right circle) Lester Parker, interpreter; (Right circle, below) Chief Thomas Yallup. At his left is sub-chief James Stahai (Klickitat).

Skookum's barn, for which the railroad paid him damages when it had to be destroyed for the right-of-way.

Louis Van Pelt Spino as a young girl with her father, the well known bootlegger.

Skookum's "Hyas Waum" sweat-house.

Skookum's grave.

Louise's home, the old schoolhouse—after the flood.

Louise dressed up in her finery and carrying a corn-husk bag.

Two of the dolls made by Sally Wahkiacus.

Sally Wahkiacus shortly before her death.

Sally's Allotment House and grandson Cody—1981.

Frank Wahkiacus, Sally's last son.

Grace Forry, seated on an Appaloosa at the Fair, all dressed up in Indian finery.

The author up on a hill across from the Planer where the bootlegger used to deliver his moonshine—1925.

XVI

The Cascade Massacre

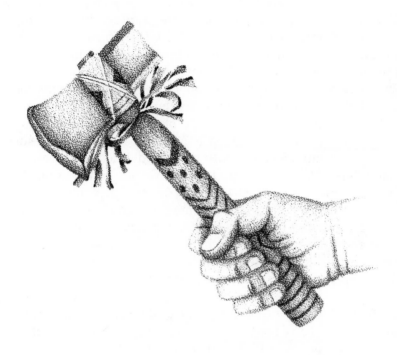

The tomahawk, one of the weapons used by the Indians in the attack.

The Cascades on the Columbia created a military hazard as well as a transportation difficulty. The long portage delayed the forwarding of military supplies that tended to accumulate there, a rich temptation for alert natives. A blockhouse had been built about midway between the two ends of the portage, but the settlements both above and below the rapids were unprotected. Two small steamers transported goods between the Cascades and The Dalles. Kamiakin, in a mood of desperation, plotted to wipe out the Cascade settlements and then move up to The Dalles to massacre and burn. He thought the propitious time to do this was when both river steamers were at the Cascades and he could burn them there. The two steamboats were lying idle at Mill Creek.

He sent in thirty Yakimas who were joined by twenty Klickitats to lead the attack. They were to kill and burn and then wait for Kamiakin to arrive with a larger force. The troops usually stationed at The Dalles had been sent to build a fort up the river, General Wool had sent two of the three companies stationed at Fort Vancouver to Steilacoom, and only nine men were left at the Cascades to protect that vulnerable place.

Everything seemed to be favorable. Peu-peu-mox-mox and Kamiakin had planned their strategy and were waiting for such an opportunity. Because both men had Klickitat wives, the daughters of Chief Ten-nak, they knew the country well. Peu-peu-mox-mox had cause to be bitter against the whites. He had sent two of his children to the mission school at Willamette, where Jason Lee had named them Lucy and Elijah Hedding, after a well known Methodist bishop. While at the school, Lucy became ill and died, but Elijah continued on for four school years, spending his summers in Yakima.

He grew into a bright young man and showed early qualities of leadership. He was his father's pride. He became a leader among the young men and was successful in leading raiding parties for horses. In 1844, at the age of seventeen, he and some other young men went to southern Oregon and northern California, stealing horses as they went along and selling them to the mountain tribes. At Sutter's Fort in California a hot headed American shot and killed Elijah while he was kneeling in prayer after a mission service. Grover Cooke, the white man who fired the shot, was never punished for the crime. This aroused great bitterness in the hearts of the chiefs, and was another reason for revenge as Peu-peu-mox-mox had not forgotten.

There are many records and personal letters telling the story of the Cascade attack, but it needs re-telling, because these were Klickitats, and if we want to understand them, we need to know how they thought and acted when they were the white man's enemies as well as friends.

A blockhouse had been built between the upper and lower landings at the Cascades, where nine men had been left to guard this post. On March 24, 1856, the main company of soldiers had left on the steamer, *Mary*. Chief Chenewuth of the Cascades sent his son's wife, a Klickitat girl, to the Klickitat village to spy on her people about their war plans and come back and tell them all that she could find out. She returned on a dark trail, no less than five miles, to report to Chief Chenewuth that the Klickitats were planning an attack. Indian Jack, Chief Chenewuth's runner and slave, was sent out to warn the white folks that the Klickitats and Yakimas were planning to kill every immigrant and to strike at the Cascades where the army's supplies were stored.

On the morning of March 26, 1856, a cold east wind was blowing and the village was just getting into the morning's activity. At this time the Klickitats and Yakimas attacked the upper landing and the blockhouse, surprising the settlers, who were unaware of their approach until they heard the cracks of the guns and the bullets striking. The settlers ran to the store for safety through a shower of fire, with one man killed and several wounded. Of the forty men, women, and children who sought refuge in the store, there were only eighteen men and four women who were able to fight.

Everything was confusion. One man took a peek out the door and was instantly killed. For two days and nights they were held under siege while others from the lower parts of the settlement were being attacked and a number were killed and wounded. Near the store several settlers, shielded from the Indians by the rocks but on view from the store, called for help, but there was no way to go to them. Those wounded who were inside the store were feverish and begged for water, but there was none in the store. Finally, a Spokane Indian volunteered, undressed, and slipped down the bank to the river and returned safely with water.

During these days and nights the Indians burned the sawmill, the warehouse, the dock, and houses, lighting up the surroundings through the nights for with the strong east winds blowing, the flames burned like holocausts. Fire brands were constantly thrown on the store roof but fell off for the most part. Those that ignited small fires were put out by using the brine from the pork barrels.

The two steam boats originally targeted by Kamiakin miraculously escaped with a few passengers. Their hoped for return with help was anxiously awaited.

Morning dawned on the third day, and lo, the *Wasco* and the *Mary*, blue with soldiers, towing a flat boat with dragoon horses, came in sight. As the steamers landed, the Indians fired twenty or thirty shots. The soldiers could not be restrained and plunged into the woods in every direction, while howitzers sent grape shot after the retreating Indians.

When a rescue boat from Fort Vancouver finally approached the lower landing, it blew its whistle to let the beleaguered folks know that help was arriving but in so doing it had alerted all the Indians, and they were gone. The soldiers could find no retreating Indians, dead or alive, up the usual trail. It was later learned that they escaped up the Wind River Valley, past the Ice Caves, and home.

Two old Klickitats, who lived into the present century and were more than one hundred years old, admitted to participating in the Cascade War. They were John Hunt, Sr., from the White Salmon Valley, who did not want to talk about it, and Jim Wahkiacus from the Klickitat River country, who would chortle with pleasure while telling his white neighbors how he had "memaloosed" the whites at the Cascades.

The whites were aroused by the atrocities. The Yakimas and the Klickitats were gone, but it was believed that the Cascade Indians had given the enemy help, even though they denied it. What irritated the settlers most was that the Indians had tortured one soldier whom they had taken prisoner, and they wanted retribution. To satisfy public feeling, local Indians were taken into custody.

One of these, Chief Chenewuth of the Cascade Indians, who stood trial under Colonel Wright, was found guilty and was sentenced to be hanged. Amos Underwood, as a volunteer, had to officiate at the hanging, even though he was a friend of Chief Chenewuth. A rope was thrown over the limb of a big cottonwood, and a whiskey barrel was set below the rope. "Kickle-stick," the chief yelled, which was his name for Amos, whom he knew and liked. His message to Amos was: "I am afraid of the white man's grave. Please put me in the death house." He was hysterical with fear. Then the chief gave to Amos, "My possessions, my two ponies, my wife Margaret, my daughter Taswaltra, and my two guns."

The barrel was kicked out and the drop was quick, but the old man had stiffened his neck so the rope didn't break his neck, and he gave out a blood curdling yell. Colonel Wright drew his pistol and shot the chief, and the crowd of onlookers was satisfied. Amos helped the family claim the body and give the chief a burial in the family death house in a cave on the north side of the river.

In the next few days seven more were hanged. A few others went off to join the Yakimas, others were imprisoned and one was reprieved on the scaffold. Thirty-one "Friendlies" went up-river to Hood River with William Jenkins, the newly appointed agent for the Indians. They promised to throw off their blankets and dress like the settlers, which most of them were doing anyway. After the promise, many of them took up homesteads, which was really buying the land back from the government — the same land they had lived on for years, but homesteading gave them the land legally. Many took new names, usually white man's names.

Both Sapot-i-well and his wife, who had worked for the Joslyns and were regarded as "Friendlies," remained with the settlers. They took the names of Bertha and Charley Johnson and were afraid to go anywhere for a long time but lived quietly in the community for many years.

The war at the Cascades had not settled anything. The Yakimas began killing travelers on the way through their country to the mines in the north. There were still no roads in the country, only Indian trails. Some killings were reported and other people simply disappeared never to be heard of again. Hatred of the Indians grew among the settlers. Many of those beginning to come into the country north of the river were afraid and thought that the Indians should be exterminated.

Kamiakin was disappointed that he was unable to consolidate the tribes behind him. He never collected any bonus, because he did not move onto the reservation, and he went north to avoid any further activity with the Yakimas.

XVII

The White Salmon Reservation

The safety of a fort was the only refuge during Indian troubles.

After the war the Joslyns stayed for some time in The Dalles, where they had a woolen mill business. They then moved down to Forest Grove until the fall of 1856, when they came back to their farm at Bingen. They were surprised to find their farm occupied as an Indian reservation under the orders of Governor Stevens of Washington Territory, who it must be remembered was also the Superintendent of Indian Affairs. A blockhouse and barns had been built, and troops were stationed to guard the Indian Agent and the Friendlies. Eight hundred peaceful Indians were kept under guard for their safety from Hostiles from

95

the fall of 1856 to the year 1859. When the Joslyns tried to live there, the agent would not permit them to do so. The farm buildings had been burned, the fruit trees pulled out, and the herd of cattle were gone, quantities of the timber had been cut for the new buildings, and cords of cottonwood had been sold to the river steamers. Joslyn felt that he had every right to his farm as he had adhered to the terms of the law before being forced off by the Indian attack. He felt the government should not only pay him rent but should also compensate him for the damage done. He gathered the signed statements of reliable persons who could report the facts of the case, such as affidavits signed by the army officers who had received orders to build a blockhouse and station troops on the claim of E. S. Joslyn. In addition, neighbors of Joslyn could testify of his residence, the damage done to his property, and that he had been deprived of the opportunity of earning an income, as he was considered to be just as good a farmer as his neighbors.

The Thirty-Sixth Congress considered a compensation to Joslyn of $1,000 for damages along with $3,000 for three years use and occupancy of his claim. The Committee on Indian Affairs reported favorably, and "To the point that the claim should be reported to the Treasury for adjudication and payment." Nothing happened. Twelve years later, on May 2, 1872, the Forty-Second Congress in their House Report No. 62 recommended passage of the bill. They reduced the rent to $2,000, saying that Joslyn had overestimated the rent for the three years. The damage amount was reduced as well.

The ruling in the Joslyn case finally came in 1922, sixty years later. The Indians complained about the slowness in the dealings with Washington; it appears the Joslyns had grounds for a similar complaint.

Few living in the area today know that the first Klickitat reservation was set up at White Salmon, where 800 Friendlies from Vancouver, Cascades, and Klickitats were protected from the warring tribes for their own safety. Those 800 persons on the reservation had to be fed during the winter. As spring advanced, their supplies were curtailed as much as possible, so that they would be willing to go to the mountains for roots and berries.

About 100 persons applied for help in gardening and were supplied with tools, which was encouraging. During the fishing season they received help to lay up stores for winter use.

At no time were they held against their will and sometimes they were urged to leave. Unless intimidated by the Hostiles, they seemed to be content to adapt to the new ways.

Honorable J. W. Nesmith was Superintendent of Indian Affairs for Washington and Oregon, and J. Cain was Indian Agent for the Columbia District. Agent Cain reported to his superior on July 29, 1857:

"I herewith transmit you my annual report for my district for the fiscal year ending June 10, 1857. It is with feelings of gratification that I have it in my power to report peace and quiet throughout my district. The country comprising this district in Washington territory bordering on the Columbia River from its mouth to the vicinity of The Dalles, having charge of all the Indians, who live on the reservation lays in Klickitat County, between the Klickitat and White Salmon Rivers; a distance of 15 miles along the Columbia River, and extended back to Camas Prairie about 20 miles, laying on the east side of the Cascade Mountains. It is well adapted for Indian use containing many wild roots, berries, game, fish in the river but poorly adapted for agricultural use. There are a few meadows that could be used for tillable crops."

The war continued spasmodically through the years, whenever there were outbreaks of massacre. The agent would retaliate with punishment. Battles followed old patterns; troops guarding supply trains as they rode, Indians dashing up or riding by and firing, troops returning fire. By August, 1858, the rifles were the new Sharps rifles. Not knowing of the much greater range of the new weapons cost the Indians dearly.

Finally, as time went on, there were few chiefs left. Kamiakin had abandoned the cause and had gone north, while Skloom and others had lost prestige and were soon forgotten.

On October 9, 1858, Colonel Wright ordered the Walla Walla to assemble. When they had gathered, he ordered all those who had taken part in the war to stand. Of the thirty-five who arose, he selected four to be hanged, in order to frighten the others.

The Walla Walla episode ended the war. By military order General Wool closed the Yakima country to settlement until the following year when General Harney succeeded Wool and re-opened the Columbia area to settlement. All these changes of policy brought confusion and mistrust.

The army of the 1850's was in the regular tradition, well organized and proud of its battle record and numbered about 15,000 in 1856. Major General John Ellis Wool, Commander of the Department of the Pacific, suggested the establishment of Fort Simcoe to replace Fort White Salmon in order to better enforce his Indian policy. He believed that the Indians would be peaceable, if left alone, and to this end he had discouraged white settlement in the area, a policy which seemed practical as the land was not considered fit for agricultural purposes. He did not approve of the volunteer system of the army as the men had too many personal grievances and were not properly trained. Of the opinion that White Salmon was too far to one side to serve well, he proposed a military post on the Toppenish Plain, close to the Naches Pass, where it would command the Indian trails to the north and to the east.

XVIII

Fort Simcoe

The commanding officers' residence at Fort Simcoe.

The military need for Fort Simcoe in August, 1856, was the old Indian problem arising from the gradual taking over of the land by the white settlers.

The Fort Simcoe site, 38 miles southwest of Yakima, had long been a favorite camping area for the tribes of the Yakima nation. The cold springs known to the Indians and called by them "Mool Mool" (bubbling water) offered plenty of water. Timber was close, and grazing areas were available. Weather in the valley was usually better than further north. Colonel Wright, commanding the Northern District, reported these advantages.

"The site is on the southern boundary of the Simcoe Valley, and at the intersection of the trails from Fort Dalles, and the Kamas Prairie . . . It is the habitation of the Klickitats . . . The point above referred to has the advantage of commanding both routes to the Columbia, and holding the Klickitats in check, who would not be likely to commit any hostile acts with a military force in their rear."

Major Robert Selden Garnett of the Ninth Infantry Regiment was chosen for the task of establishing Fort Simcoe, and by the end of summer Major Garnett and two companies began preparing accommodations for four companies. Since all materials were to come from Fort Dalles, 65 miles away, there was need for a better road. During August and September a wagon road from Fort Dalles to Simcoe was built to accommodate the army wagons bringing in loads of supplies. During the winter when the road was unfit for travel, pack trains came in on a lower road along the Yakima River. Only a limited amount of goods could be brought in that first season, which meant that Garnett had to resort to local supplies. As a result, the first buildings were of hewed logs and whipsawn boards of pine cut within five miles of the Fort.

Arrangement of the buildings at Fort Simcoe was similar to that found at most military posts. The buildings were placed around a parade ground 420 feet square. The upper portion of the square was enclosed by the officers' quarters and the lower half by barracks, storehouses, guardhouses, and a hospital building. Directly behind these buildings were the servants' and laundresses' quarters, kitchens, and messrooms. The four officers' quarters were impressive buildings with the commandant's residence really elegant. While the buildings were less ambitious than Garnett had wished, they were far more luxurious than others found at military posts in the wilderness.

From reports and correspondence it is evident that Major Garnett's plans were more ambitious than those his army superiors had contemplated. It must have been a stupendous problem to build in primitive wilderness without fit roads and only army personnel for workmen. He did, however, have an architect who was a lay person and who left his mark on The Dalles buildings as well as Simcoe's.

Even today when one visits the restored Fort Simcoe, one marvels at the diamond shaped window panes, the large fireplaces, and the interesting furniture. Because Garnett was to marry a New York girl, he wanted to provide a nice place for her to live, knowing she would be lonely with only soldiers and Indians and possibly another woman or two for company, if the other officers would bring their wives. Major Garnett knew he would be gone most of the time keeping the Indians under control.

Many of Mrs. Garnett's letters still remain to tell of life at the fort. Tragedy struck when she and her seven-month-old son died of "bilious fever" while Garnett was out on a tour of duty. When Garnett came back to Fort Simcoe after the deaths of his wife and son, he applied for leave and in October, 1856, left Simcoe with the bodies, never to return. During the Civil War Garnett fought with the South and reached the rank of Brigadier General in the Confederate Army.

Captain James J. Archer followed Major Garnett as commanding officer at Fort Simcoe. The fort was nearing its last days, and in March, 1859, they learned that the post was to be abandoned. As long as white settlement was to be excluded from the country east of the Cascades in accordance with General Wool's orders and upheld by his successor General Newman S. Clarke, Fort Simcoe had a military purpose to fulfill. In the fall of 1858 Brigadier General W. W. Harney succeeded to the command of the recently created Department of the Columbia, or Oregon, and he reversed the policy of Wool and Clarke. He withdrew the prohibition on settlement east of the Cascades and proposed the measure that led to the abandonment of Fort Simcoe.

On May 22, 1859, Fort Simcoe was turned over to the Department of Indian Affairs, and an agency that had been established at the mouth of the White Salmon was moved to the Simcoe site. The conversion of the post into an Indian agency would be of help for further military action in case of trouble. The site was particularly suited for agency purposes because "Mool Mool" had long been a meeting place for Indian camps.

Simcoe, as their agency headquarters, became an important influence in the life of the Klickitats. The White Salmon Reservation was moved in the spring of 1859 and the Agent Lansdale brought 147 Klickitats from the Lewis River. Work was started on gardens, cattle were brought in, and a sawmill was under construction when Lansdale was suspended on "serious charges." In reality there seem to have been some grounds for charges, but a confusion existed over authority of territorial officers and their jurisdictions. Moreover, payments for employees did not come through with regularity, and some had gone without pay.

A school, which had been promised in the treaty, was in operation for the first time and was under the supervision of Rev. James H. Wilbur, assisted by Mr. Wright and lady. There were fifteen boys and three girls in daily attendance.

The agency was not well managed, and President Lincoln appointed Ashley Bancroft. This political appointment, too, proved a failure.

Leaders of the various bands of Indians were disturbed, reporting that their annuities were dwindling and by the second year had become so small that they were not worth making the trip to the agency. The Indians held the Reverend Wilbur in high respect and confided in him. When he attempted to reason with Bancroft, he was discharged. In a letter two days later he asked permission to remain without expense as teacher, but his request was denied. Trouble continued under Bancroft until Wilbur went to Washington, as the story goes. He laid his protests before President Lincoln, who appointed him agent, and he served in that position for eighteen years.

Father Wilbur, as he came to be known, had a great influence on the life of the Indians. It is well known the kind of man he was. When he arrived in Portland in 1837, there were thirteen houses in a dense forest. He was a Methodist minister and his circuit, with headquarters at Salem, reached out southward for twenty-five miles over the width of the Willamette Valley. He multiplied himself by means of Cayuse ponies and preached wherever he found a listener. Many rough mountain men and neglected immigrants were led to a Christian life by his preaching. While at Salem he taught at the Oregon, now Willamette, University. In 1849 he was appointed to the Oregon City and Portland circuit of the church.

In 1850 his work resulted in establishment of the first Portland church, and the next year in the formation of the Portland Academy, where he took a hand in the actual labor — wearing a striped shirt, mixing mortar, and carrying hods. After two years he became presiding elder of the Umpqua District of Southern Oregon. Here from 1853 to 1857 he lived through the Rogue gold fever and two Indian wars. During the uprisings he went wherever and whenever he was wanted and was never harmed.

"They did not harm me," he said, "because I was not armed. I have had, I believe, more experience with Indians than any man in the past and I never have carried a knife, pistol, nor any other weapon; nor did I ever have occasion to defend myself, and have never been injured by them."

His next move was in 1857, to a position as presiding elder of the Willamette District. He speculated in real estate and made some money.

In 1859 Father Wilbur paid a visit to his field in the "wilds" east of the mountains. At The Dalles he bought a Cayuse Pony, which ran off and left him to cross the Blue Mountains on the march for fifty-four hours without a meal. At Walla Walla he organized a church of seven members; the city then consisted of five houses. Once, while he was preaching, some of the rough men of the place held a cattle auction within fifty feet of him, so that he had to make his sermon heard above the shouting auctioneer.

This was the man who in 1860 began to work for the Indians. His work became recognized throughout the United States.

The Indians on the reservation surrounding Fort Simcoe had grown sullen and dissatisfied after the treaty and did not take kindly toward civilization. They had waited until 1859 for Congress to sign the treaty and the government's promises had not been kept. There had been an unfortunate choice of agents and their management; Kamiakin had left and the Indians were without powerful leadership.

With the advent of Wilbur, agency work and reports immediately began to take on business-like organization. He built up the attendance in the school. The girls were taught to sew and cook besides learning to read and write, as well as some Bible teaching. The boys learned gardening and plowing with oxen. They were particularly interested in the care of cattle and were adept at it.

Wilbur outlawed liquor runners on the reservation and was a strict disciplinarian who even resorted to the whipping post (for women as well as men). The ball and chain were used for punishment for non-Indian offenders. He was the law of the land when Simcoe was the leading settlement of the area.

There was the time, one crackling cold January, a military escort herded onto the Yakima Reservation 543 Snake and Paiute Indians, without any official notice of their coming. They were brought from Fort Henry and the disbanded Malheur Reservation in Oregon. They had resisted settlement for so long and had become scattered and prowling bands attacking wagon trains. They arrived on the Yakima reservation nearly naked, almost starved, and in a destitute condition. Something had to be done immediately as it was freezing weather. Wilbur wired the Commissioner of Indian Affairs for help, as the Yakima rations were sparse. He put the Yakimas to work to cut and haul lumber to build a shelter, 150 feet long and 17 feet wide. This camp was on Toppenish Creek, seven miles east of Simcoe. One wonders, in this day of insulation ads, just how much shelter there was from that cold, windy, and snowy weather.

Sarah Winnemucca was one of the refugees and Wilbur hired her as an interpreter and teacher, later replacing her with Rev. George Waters. Both of these Indians had made names for themselves throughout the whole area. They had gone from tribe to tribe to teach the Indians the hopelessness of combating the whites. Rev. Waters was the Rev. Stwire, of whom it was written earlier that he was the adopted son of The Dalles missionaries who had rescued him from death. Sarah, the daughter of the old Chief Winnemucca, seemingly content at first, took issue with Wilbur and went to Washington, D.C., to complain to the Commissioner of Indian Affairs about cold, wet camps, the wide-spread deaths of her people, and the lack of clothing and food. In her lifetime, no doubt, she did much good, but she also brought ill-will and trouble.

At first the Yakimas at Simcoe had regarded the Paiutes as guests needful of assistance. They willingly consented to withdrawals from the Yakima rations, and at Christmas they slaughtered cattle, gathered presents of food and clothing, and delivered them to the Paiute camp.

In a few years they were given permission to leave. Sarah spread the story that they were kept as a source of riches for Wilbur and that he starved them and sold the supplies. She did not tell of the Paiutes refusing to work to make their own future secure as the Yakimas were doing. Her own people finally turned against her, and she died after growing old and friendless. Even her two marriages with Army men were forgotten.

Many times Wilbur was accused of being unduly partial to those Indians, who told him that they wanted to become Christians and learn the religion that he taught. Be that as it may, the white people who knew him felt that he was very fair and just. It is easy to criticize anyone who seems to be accomplishing a task worthwhile.

At this time many of the tribes east of the Cascades began practicing a religion that was known as the Dreamers. It originated in the tribe of the Wi-nah-pams, or Priest Rapids Indians, under the leadership of Smo-hal-la, a strong and cunning character. As soon as he took over, he organized the religion, basing it on the ceremony used by a former chieftain who had gained a reputation as a prophet.

Smo-hal-la was a medicine man supposedly making bad medicine to bring about the death of the head of their neighboring tribe, Chief Moses, who became frightened and decided to rid himself of the threat. He met Smo-hal-la one day, set upon and beat him until he thought Smo-hal-la was dead, and left him.

But Smo-hal-la was not dead. He revived, crawled to the river where he lay down in a canoe, and floated down the river. Some white people below Umatilla found him and cared for him until he could travel. Not wanting to return because he knew Moses would kill him the next time they met, he began one of the most unusual wanderings ever made by an uncivilized Indian, traveling all around the Southwest and as far as Mexico. He was gone for two years, and his people supposed him dead. Upon his return he announced that he had been in the Spirit World but had been sent back to warn his people not to accept any of the ways of the palefaces. His doctrine was opposed to civilization. His people raised no food of any kind, had no cattle, sheep, hogs, or chickens, not even vegetables. Their food consisted only of fish, game, roots, and berries. He said, "My young men shall never work, for men who work cannot dream, and wisdom comes from dreams. We will not plow the ground, for we cannot tear up our Mother's breast. We will cut no hay, for we dare not cut off our Mother's hair."

When he came into prominence, he was a middle aged man with a fine face that was always wreathed in smiles, but he was a hunchback, a very unusual deformity among the Indians. The Indians believed he had rare mystical powers. His sessions were always accompanied by the hypnotic beating of the tom-toms, dancing, and the singing of war songs. This would continue until everyone would be in a frenzy and then things often got out of control.

The dream habit seemed to be catching and spread to the neighboring tribes. An old scalawag named Colwash, on the north bank of the Columbia across from The Dalles, got the fever, and at that place dreams and dancing commenced. It was reported to Father Wilbur who sent word to Colwash that this had to stop, and to close up his dance house. Colwash chose not to hear and the dreams and the dancing continued. Wilbur sent two Indian policemen to arrest Colwash, but the tribesmen crowded so closely around the performer that the policemen could not get near him and had to come away without making an arrest.

They made their report to Wilbur, who was just finishing his dinner. After listening quietly to them, he turned to an attendant and ordered a team to be hitched to his two-seated hack, ready for an immediate start to the Grand Dalles.

To Mrs. Wilbur, he said, "Mother, a little lunch for our supper."

Inside of an hour, accompanied by his two unsuccessful policemen, Father Wilbur was on his way. He never carried a gun, but he was a man of powerful physique, kind-hearted and generous, but sternly just and utterly fearless.

Late that night he reached the blockhouse at Spring Creek, fifty miles from Fort Simcoe and thirty miles from Grand Dalles. He rested there until morning. With a fresh team he reached Colwash's camp before noon and found the dance in full swing, with the tom-toms beating time to their war songs.

Springing from the hack, he walked to the door of the dance hall where nearly the whole band of Indians had gathered as soon as they saw him. They tried at once to block his way, just as they had in the case of the two policemen. Then trouble began. He flailed out with his two long arms, pitching the obstructors this way and that. They were soon tumbling over each other while trying to get out of the way of those powerful punches.

With the road cleared, Father Wilbur snatched the wily old Dreamer by the nape of the neck, literally yanking him out of the house, head foremost. Then he handcuffed the old trouble maker, picked him up bodily, plopped him into the back seat of the hack, and took a place by his side. Jeers and laughter had followed the Indian policemen a few days earlier, when they left empty handed, but there were no jeers or laughter as Father Wilbur drove off on his way back to Fort Simcoe.

Father Wilbur knew that if peace was to be maintained, there could be no more of these wild "get togethers" that roused the Indians to war. If a little liquor was added, the problem became even greater.

Another interesting episode took place over on Rock Creek where Mr. Chapman and a companion were herding sheep. When Mr. Chapman had settled in Klickitat County in 1878, Indians were on the rampage in Oregon and Idaho, which alarmed the settlers in Washington. In fact, most of them had gone to The Dalles or Goldendale for safety. One day when the men were busy with the sheep, a band of renegade Klickitats surrounded them. For four days the men were held prisoners, until their relief was accomplished by Father Wilbur, who came unarmed from Fort Simcoe, held a pow-wow with the Indians, and succeeded in dispersing them.

The old settlers would tell of the camp meetings Father Wilbur used to hold under the cottonwoods along Klickitat Creek in Goldendale, bringing some of the Simcoe Indians with him. With women and children sitting on one side of a semi-circle and the men on the other, they would hold services lasting for several days. Both red and white enjoyed the singing and fellowship.

By 1878, under Wilbur, Simcoe Indians had built up a good herd of cattle, branded with an "ID" (Indian Department), through purchase and increase. The Indians, as individuals, owned as many as 16,000 head of horses besides the cattle. With things going so well for the Indians, the Indian agencies were insensibly turned back to the military department, whose first move was to sell the band of "ID" cattle. A. J. Splawn, the cattleman, said, "I purchased the greater part of them myself. If any benefit was ever derived from the ill advised sale of the useful herd of Indian cattle, it never showed up on the Simcoe Reservation. Fortunately for the Indians, the rotten military administration did not last long. About the only thing it succeeded in was the partial undoing of Father Wilbur's good work and the debauching of a few native women."

Another Indian scare that happened back in 1866 was at the J. Chapman place on Rock Creek. The Chapmans had a little Indian boy staying with them, and they were in the habit of sending him out every evening to drive up the horses. They also had a boy of their own about the same age as the Indian boy. The Indian boy did not consider it fair that he was the one who had to get the horses, while the son remained comfortably at home, and so he made a complaint to Jane, the Chapman daughter. All the satisfaction she gave him was a sound cuffing on the ears, a treatment which perhaps did not hurt him much but thoroughly roused his temper. He went to other Indians camped nearby, told them his story of abuse, and stirred them to violent action. The Indians, determined to slaughter the whole family, went with loaded guns directly to the Chapman home and made their attack. In the fight that ensued, one Indian shot at Jane, but the bullet ricocheted and did not pierce her skull. After its removal the girl soon recovered. One of the Indians, called Chief George, was shot through the body and slashed with a sword. The man who attacked George with the sword was a migrant staying at the home and the sword was a Civil War sword that had hung on the wall as a decoration. Chief George was left for dead, but recovered and lived another year or so.

XIX

Young Joseph

Chief Joseph could not persuade the Klickitats and Yakimas to join him in his war against the whites.

In 1877 the Government was still trying to settle Indians onto reservations. However, young Joseph and his people of the Nez Perce did not want to leave their valley, not only because it was home, but because they were horsemen with wealth that they prized in their thousands of horses. Many of these horses were Blue Appaloosas with five-fingered spotted rumps, that had become their pride for hunting and for war. The Government was assigning twenty-acre allotments to heads of families, not enough to sustain their horses. But to avoid a hopeless clash with the American authorities, Joseph at last agreed to take his people out of the Wallowa Valley and settle on the Lapwai Reservation as the government wanted them to do.

To complicate matters, some white neighbors took this opportunity to make away with several hundred of the Indian horses while the Nez Perce were getting ready to move. The Indians, already heartsick, homesick, and angered, counted their grievances until the moment came when they could be restrained no longer. In an attack for revenge, a party of a few men murdered eighteen settlers. The troops arrived. After all those years of peace, Joseph asked in vain for help from the Yakimas and Klickitats. Joseph, who had said, "...rather than have war, I would give up my country...I would give up everything..." no longer had any other choice. He took men, women, and children on that famous retreat that kept our army generals in pursuit until almost within sight of his goal.

In the absence of written records from Nez Perce headquarters it will never be possible to give credit for various battle plans, but it is certain that the orders for "No Scalping" and "Captive Women Freed" were due to Joseph.

His surrender was one of the most dramatic events of any Indian war. Dismounting from his horse, he advanced with his right hand extended in a sign of peace and said, "Tell General Howard I knew his heart. What he told me before in Idaho I have in my heart. I am tired of fighting...My people ask me for food and I have none to give. It is cold and we have no blankets, no wood. My people are starving to death. Hear me, my Chiefs, I fought, but from where the sun now stands, Joseph will fight no more."

He drew his blanket over his face after the Indian custom when in mourning or humiliated, and instead of walking back to his people, he walked directly into the line of army officers, a prisoner.

He had been promised that his people could go back to the Wallowas but, instead, they were sent to the malaria-infested district in Indian territory. Here his six children and many of the band died. Eventually, they were allowed to come back to the Northwest, but not to the Wallowas, as promised him at the surrender. Instead they were sent where no supplies had been provided and their suffering was great.

General Miles said, "I think that in his long career, Joseph cannot accuse the Government of the United States of one single act of Justice."

The Nez Perce experiences affected all the tribes and filled the Indians with a lack of respect and trust in the white man's word.

The war of 1877 had taken place at too great a distance from the Klickitats and Yakimas to affect them physically; however an Indian war and the perception of white injustice always caused uneasiness and excitement among the tribes, even those hundreds of miles from the hostilities.

Perkins' Massacre

The lonely marker of a tragic event.

But there was one incident in 1877 that caused the settlers to seek safety in the blockhouses and towns. It was the senseless atrocity committed just outside the new Klickitat County boundary when Perkins and his wife were murdered. During the excitement that followed this event, all kinds of rumors were afloat, and every movement made by the Indians was held suspicious. The position of Chief Moses in the affair was far from clear, though he continued to disclaim any responsibility in the affair. Blame fell upon the outlaw Umatilla renegades who he vowed were not in any way connected with his band. The whole country became alarmed. During the height of the excitement in the Yakima Valley the settlers had banded together in many places. In the Glenwood area the settlers had listened to Dr. Homlik, the medicine man, and sought the blockhouse in the Klickitat Valley. Some gathered at the blockhouse on Spring Creek, and others went to Goldendale, where Enoch Pike organized the only voluntary military company in the territory for home defense at the time of the Bannock and Paiute War, which had sixty members on its muster roll.

The outlaw Umatillas fighting the whites on the south side of the Columbia were a small group escaping from the military. Their crossing of the Columbia was to be the signal for the hostile Klickitats, Yakimas, and other tribes to attack. When some of this band of Indians crossed the Columbia, a steamer, which had been converted to a gun boat, began firing, killing several and keeping a larger group from crossing. Among those crossing successfully were: Wi-ah-ne-cat, Sch-lus-kin, Te-wow-ne, Chick-chuck-moas-tonic, Ta-nah-hop-tow-ne, Kipe, and others, including some of the worst renegades in the whole Northwest who were on their way north.

These outlaws reached the Rattlesnake Springs just outside the new Klickitat County border and there came upon Mr. and Mrs. Perkins, who were on their way to visit Mrs. Perkins' mother and where Mrs. Perkins would stay for the birth of her child. They had left their cabin on the east side of the Columbia River that morning, being ferried over by a neighbor. To understand what happened next it is best to follow the story as recorded in the book, *Kamiakin*, by A. J. Splawn, the well-known cattleman and author, who was friendly to the Indians and acted as interpreter at the trial. Each and every one of the Indians told practically the same story, convicting themselves without testimony.

"When they found the man and his wife at the springs, Wi-ah-ne-cat suggested they kill them. Ta-nah-hop-tow-ne was willing as two of his own people had been killed by the gun boat, and one of them had been a friend of his. He wanted revenge. First, they wanted to see if Perkins was armed so they went to them and asked for food. The Perkins' gave them nearly all they had as they expected to reach Yakima City that night.

"During this conversation, Mr. and Mrs. Perkins, no doubt became alarmed and began to saddle their horses. Wi-ah-ne-cat and Ta-nah-hop-tow-ne drew their guns and ordered Perkins to stop. He had his own horse saddled by this time and mounted. Mrs. Perkins did not wait to saddle but mounted her mare bareback and with only a rope around the horse's neck to guide her, started on the run. A shot from Ta-nah-hop-tow-ne's gun wounded Perkins, but he kept on until a shot from Wi-ah-ne-cat reached him and he fell from his horse and soon died.

"Mrs. Perkins' horse now began to out distance her pursuers, when a deep ravine appeared, which the brave little mare failed to clear. The animal fell, throwing her rider who lay stunned until the Indians came up. She raised her hands, they said, as if in prayer. Then begged them if they must kill someone to let it be her, and to save her husband, she not knowing that he was already dead. While the Indians who had come up to Mrs. Perkins sat upon their horses undecided, Wi-ah-ne-cat came up and asked why they sat there like women, instead of killing her and he promptly drew his gun and killed her. So died Blanche Bunting Perkins, her young life cut short by a fiendish renegade out on the lonely hills of the Rattlesnakes."

By the terms of the original treaty the Indians of this band belonged to the Simcoe Reservation, but they had never lived there, always living with smaller bands along the Columbia between the mouth of the Umatilla and Wishram at Celilo. The crime, therefore, was not just chargeable to the Yakimas.

Agent Wilbur, upon appeal for assistance, sent out three Indian scouts and six white men who found the remains of Mr. and Mrs. Perkins in a ravine, covered with rocks. It looked as if Mrs. Perkins had been buried before death and this roused the whites even more. Feeling ran high, and it was felt that Chief Moses was befriending the renegades, even though he vowed to his innocence.

A volunteer group was raised to find Moses. They moved down the river to Smohalla's village of fifty lodges, but only old men, women and children were found. The fighting men, no doubt, had gone out with Moses. The volunteers kept watch at night and captured Moo-tonic, one of the murderers. Having learned that the rest of the renegades with a considerable force were fortified in the lava beds at Crab Creek, they got more volunteers at Yakima City. The combined forces approached, and they were surprised to hear Moses call out to Splawn not to shoot. Splawn ordered the camp surrounded but not to shoot. When Moses and nine of the followers were made prisoners and disarmed, it was with difficulty that Splawn prevented his men from shooting Moses.

Moses gave the excuse for being so far from home to be his discovery of the hiding place of the murderers and his wish to guide the white men to them. Moses was anxious and asked Captain Splawn what they would do with him. To which Captain Splawn replied that no decision had been made.

Whereupon Moses, powerful a man as he was, cried and said he regretted the way he had acted. This is surprising as we are always told about the stoicism of the Indians.

Moses, in cooperation with Captain Splawn, sent sixteen of his warriors after the murderers. They returned with Ta-nah-hop-tow-ne, and reported another had committed suicide. The prisoners, including Moses, were then taken into Yakima City, where Captain Pike's militia company from Goldendale was called to guard the jail as it was feared that some of the citizens were so enraged that they might try to break in the jail and hang the Indians.

At the request of Agent Wilbur, the Klickitat militia escorted Moses from Yakima City to the agency at Fort Simcoe, for safety. One member of Captain Pike's own company made an attempt to kill the chief, but the click of the rifle warned the captain, and the man was quickly disarmed.

Moses remained at the agency until February 1879, when he was permitted to start for home on the Columbia. On reaching Yakima, he was arrested on a warrant charging him with complicity in the murder of Mr. Perkins and his wife. He was tried, released on bonds furnished by Wilbur and allowed to proceed on his way.

Soon afterward Moses was called to Washington, D.C., where he succeeded in getting a large reservation set aside for his tribe on the west side of the Okanagan River, a gift which he never would have received had it not been for the notoriety he gained in connection with the Perkins' murder. It was the mistaken policy of the government to make heroes out of warlike chieftains, thus paying a bonus for hostilities.

A. J. Splawn had always believed Moses' story, and that when he said he wanted no more war, that was his true sentiment, not because he had any love for the whites, but because he was clever enough to realize that the whites were too powerful for the Indians to cope with.

The search for the murderers had been a long one, and all except Hop-tow-ne had been accounted for: one had been allowed his liberty on account of turning state's evidence, one committed suicide, one had been killed in an effort to escape arrest and another in an effort to break jail, two had been hanged, and the seventh one met his death at the hands of James Taggart and, ironically, Robert Bunting, Mrs. Perkins' brother.

However, it was not only the Indians who committed deeds of cruelty. The settlers at Glenwood and Gilmer used to tell a tale handed down to them by the Indians; whether authentic or not, no one can say. Oregon volunteers chasing a band of Indians came upon their camp in the Goose Lake area after a heavy snowfall. The volunteers surprised the Indians by shooting into the teepees; a few trying to escape in the heavy snow were killed, adults and children were axed to death, and babies were taken by their heels and bashed against a tree. These early volunteers had many virtues, but compassion toward an Indian was not one of them.

The whites were afraid of the Indian encampments where, with their wild drumming and dancing, the Indians worked themselves into a frenzy and anything could happen. A. J. Splawn tells of an experience that happened to him while he was still a young man working for his brother and Major Thorp driving cattle. Coming into camp late one evening at Loup Creek on the Okanagan River they found a large encampment of Indians covering a flat of more than a hundred acres. Hundreds of horses grazed on the hillsides, while swift riders dashed here and there keeping individual bands separated from the others. The neighing of the horses, the barking of dogs, whooping, yelling, and wailing, along with the cries of those watching the gamblers and horse racing, made one grand tumult, the like of which he had never seen before. The only thing lacking to make this a redman's inferno was firewater. It was so nearly dark that they had been forced to camp near the village, even though their Indian herders protested.

Splawn describes it in his book on Kamiakin. "The cattle were turned loose to graze up the river. After supper our Indians took the horses into a bend of the river to guard during the night, but they got no sleep. For a while everything was quiet, then suddenly the sound of the great war drum rang out on the night; wild whoops and piercing yells showed that the war dance was on." Splawn was young and anxious to see it, but he knew that Major Thorp would not allow it, so he stole away without telling him, worked through the Indians, sometimes crawling, sometimes running until he reached the great wigwam where the warriors were having a wild dance. He says, "As fascinating a sight as I ever beheld was my first war dance." But after a while just looking on did not satisfy him. To be one of them was the call of the wild that made him worm his way into the circle, catching the rhythm, his long yellow hair streaming behind. He was soon swaying and chanting with the best of them.

"Suddenly I was conscious that the other dancers had withdrawn to one end of the room, leaving me alone in the center. Whether to run or stand my ground became a serious problem, but only that day the Major had said, 'Don't show the white feather and you will win the Indian's respect nine times out of ten.' So I stuck to my dancing, and a blessed thing it was that I was ignorant of the tremendous risk I was running.

"After a short parlay the dance went on as before. A scalp fastened to a rope was brought in, thrown in the ring, then trailed in the dust. Men and women jumped on it and kicked it with their feet. That gruesome plaything had belonged to a white man's head, for these Indians were not at war with any other tribe then and had not been for some time; and the scalp was fresh and with short hair." As it came close to him, he wondered whose head it had covered and whose would furnish the next one. The thought sobered him, so while they were in a frenzy, he slipped out to the camp, where he received one of the severest lectures of his life.

"We were up early," he goes on. "We found the cattle a short distance up the river and had driven them several miles before we counted them. To my chagrin, the Major reported, 'six head shy but we were lucky at that.' I didn't look at it that way. I was mad to think that we had let a bunch of breech-clouts steal from us. When I made a proposition to go back after them, they all refused to go with me, thinking more of their cowardly hides than of the six steers. I wheeled my horse and lit back on the trail. I had gone only a few miles when I spied twenty Indians driving our cattle toward their camp. Hurrying along, I rode in front of the cattle to turn them back, but it was no time at all before it dawned on me that twenty could do more driving than one. Those cattle had become like friends to me and my mind was made up to have them. Whip in hand, I rode into their midst, striking siwashes in all directions, hitting as many as possible. The Indians rode off to a hill and did not follow me. The Major shook his head when informed of my proceedings and warned me not to do it again."

Wilbur wrote his resignation as agent on August 15, 1882. After living in Goldendale for a time, he eventually moved to Walla Walla, where he spent considerable time answering correspondence because even then long reports were required.

He died in October, 1887, when he was 76 years old, and Mrs. Wilbur died shortly after. She had been his constant companion and much admired by the Indian women.

The Settlers

A little settlers cabin to protect the newcomers from weather and Indian attacks.

There is no record of any white person losing his life in Klickitat County, but many were the occasions when the settlers expected it to happen. Many of the men had to earn cash away from home so as to have money for supplies. They found work cutting and hauling wood for the Columbia River steam boats, which depended on local supplies of wood as fuel. Some found work at The Dalles, some herded cattle or sheep. They would do any work that might bring in some funds. In 1888 it is recorded that there were 86,000 sheep in the county; apparently many sheepherders were needed.

All this meant that the women and children were left at home to manage alone. It was common to see the ugly face of a buck peering through a window, as the Indians thought the windows must be put in for the purpose of looking in as well as out. Or to turn from the stove to find that an Indian had entered on moccasined feet to see what was cooking. The children were always scared and hid under the beds or behind their mother's skirts. It may be true that the Indians were not trying to kill anyone, but it was almost as bad when they came in and ate or took the scarce food from the hungry family. Fresh bread was a great attraction, and they must have been able to smell it fresh from the oven for miles, as they always seemed to know when it was ready to eat. One settler's wife tells of having taken a crock of baked beans out of the oven for her half starved family's treat, only to have an old buck slip in and take the crock and all, leaving nothing for the family to eat.

A good example of a settler's relations with his Indian neighbors was told by C. T. Gizentanner. The story is as follows:

"When we came to the Horseshoe Bend the principal industry was stock raising, and Eastern Washington had many cattle kings. But by the following spring after the hard winter of 1881, they were paupers and it was hard to breathe from the stench going up from the thousands of cattle lying dead over the prairies. On inquiry, when we arrived, we were told that the winters were open and the stock made their living grazing, but that winter it began snowing early. It kept on till it reached a depth of six feet and remained at that depth for three months and for that time the sun was blotted out. Father, relying on the information he received, was in no hurry to lay in his winter's supplies and continued working until we were pretty low on provisions. He finally made up his mind to make a trip to The Dalles and bring home a wagonload. The morning he was to start there was two feet of snow on the ground and it was coming down 'like feathers from molting angels.' He thought it would soon stop but it didn't. We soon ran out of food. He possessed an old muzzle loading rifle with a quantity of powder, lead and caps, but being a semi-invalid from his service in the Civil War and the children all small, there was not a chance for him to get to use it as all the game had taken to the Big Klickitat Canyon. When we were existing on boiled wheat an Indian staggered against the door. He was crying. Father welcomed him to the fireside and fed him. When he had gained sufficient strength, he told a pitiful tale of suffering and want. He said there were six families of Indians living between the mouth of the Little Klickitat and the Soda Springs up on the Big Klickitat. They were starving with lots of deer around them. It appeared the only arms they had were bows and arrows, and as the snow was so deep, they couldn't get close enough to shoot them, but if they only had a gun their lives could be saved. Father gave him the muzzle loading rifle and the ammunition he had and told him to take it and save themselves, and that as to himself it was useless to him anyway. The Indian took it and hurried away.

"The incident was forgotten in our home but not so with the Indian. We had three sacks of wheat and before half of the first sack had been consumed, we saw a black speck moving across the snow about a mile away. It came plodding, especially as the Indian was on snowshoes and loaded down with deer hams. From that time on, we never missed a meal all winter. One time, however, we lost out on one trip and we all decided that he had more than paid for the gun and would not return. It wouldn't be but short time until all the wheat was gone. Now my mother and grandmother were real pioneers and for themselves would not have uttered a word, but when they thought of the children starving, the tears rolled down one of their faces and then the other one gave way to quiet weeping.

"Up to that time no wild life had been around the house. Father slipped away quietly and entered the bedroom and locked himself in and kneeling down he told God in plain English that he had done his best and that if He (God) did not come to the rescue we would all perish. While he was praying, and before he said Amen, the children were out in the yard picking up prairie chickens. They were raining down all around the doorsteps. It was a large flock that had become snow blind and in flying over had broken their wings against the tree limbs. They were the only ones during the whole winter.

"When these had about all been eaten by the hungry family, the Indian came back on his regular schedule. He said the winter had been so long that the cougars had come down off the mountain and had chased the deer farther up the Big Klickitat, away from the Indian shelters and it had taken him longer to overtake them.

"The following spring, Father started a Sunday School and all the Indians attended and took dinner at our homestead in Horseshoe Bend."

Through the experiences of the settlers, one learns what the Indians as people were really like. There were those who were kind and trustworthy just as among the whites, while a few were belligerent and not to be trusted. No doubt, commissions, congresses, councils, and committees have their place, but it is in the personal conduct of everyday life that one sees the real character of both red and white.

Some of the early Glenwood families got to know their Indian neighbors well. The settlers who moved into this Mount Adams country used Indians to transport their goods up the rough trails along the White Salmon, and several tell of losing a horse laden with an iron cook stove in the flood waters of the Rattlesnake at Husum. The Indians knew the trails and had the horses so it was a help to both, as the Indians earned small fees for the transportation.

Cody Chapman, raised in the Camas Valley, told the story of the old medicine man, Dr. Hamlik, who lived near the Chapman house at Laurel, and was Cody's frequent companion. Cody learned to speak the Indian language and to know much of the Indian's ways with roots and herbs.

"The Indian doctor," said Cody, "had a daughter and son that had died and were buried at Memaloose Island. In 1875 he was going over there for a big feed. Father and Mother let me go any place with him. A lot of Indians were there. They had a large place made of poles and grass mats, with rush and grass mats on the sand. At that time they would set the dead up all around the place they had built, together with blankets, beads, arrowheads, and other things the dead had liked, such as rock pipes. These were black and also nicely smoothed. On the stem these would be carved, then wrapped with skunk cabbage leaves, then through a small hole hot silver would be poured; it would run through the crevices and make different images. I have watched them make lots of them.

"On Memaloose Island, they also had another big round building made of poles stuck down in the sand and slanted about half pitch, with rush mats up about twelve feet high. There would be one peeled pole in the center. A chief would dance around that pole and sing till it looked like he was tired out, sweating, singing, and dancing, he would keep at it until he had nothing on but a sash. All the other Indians, women, and children kept back about ten feet, dancing around him, circling to the right with their shoulders touching; the next row just close enough to pass circling to the left, all in a circle, all dancing at once and singing. Two men, lying on a mat, would be beating drums. The drums looked like big sieves with hide stretched over them.

"After the dance would come a big supper. They would wait on the dead first; set camas, salmon, all kinds of dried berries, souweet, pine nuts, wild onions, Indian asparagus, and lots of other wild grass roots before each dead Indian.

"In the spring of 1882, the Indian Doctor Hamlik went to Celilo to fish for salmon. He was to be gone one week. After the week, we were looking for him to return when some of his Indian and white friends saw a spotted horse on Bourdoin Mountain, running loose on the range wearing a saddle. My father, Noah Chapman, identified the horse, then everyone was on the lookout for the doctor. He was found a week later, when local people noticing buzzards flying around, went looking and smelled something dead. They found he had been killed, thrown over the bluff, and his body had lodged on an oak limb. The people at Bingen suspected two brothers had done it. They were arrested and taken before the justice of the peace, but, for lack of evidence they were set free. The justice of the peace was notified by the agency at Simcoe to have the two brothers and the mother brought in. They were questioned and the mother of the two pleaded guilty. She said she had killed him and thrown him over the bluff because he had doctored some of her people and killed them, and as that was the belief of the Indians, nothing more was done about it."

Hundreds of acres of the valley were in meadows made marshy by the runoff water from Mount Adams and its surrounding hills draining off into the valley in spring. As the season progressed the water would disappear by drainage and evaporation and the settlers would cut the two- to two-and-a-half-foot wild grass for hay. Camas grew throughout the meadow, and it was one of the camas root gathering places for the Indians. While a settler was mowing the hay, the squaws were gathering camas. The mower would block off a square and cut around it. The squaws were warned to go where the mower had already cut, but it was easier for them to see the dried stalks of the camas flowers among the grass, and they refused to cooperate. Once, when one of the squaws took after the settler with her camas root digging tool, he took it away from her, broke it, and threw it in the grass and went on mowing. The women went to the house where the mother and children were and threatened to kill them with rocks. Two Indian men from a nearby wagon came to the house and made the squaw leave with them. No one wanted to test the Indians to see if the threats were real or merely efforts to scare the whites into compliance.

One day a settler and his wife, who had taken their flock of sheep some distance away to graze an early green hillside, were staying in a deserted little shack. While her husband was occupied with the sheep, she began to make supper on the decrepit wood stove, and as she was lighting the lamp, she felt hands on her shoulders. There just behind her was an ugly-looking buck. she let out some unearthly screams that not only frightened her husband up on the hillside but scared the Indian so that he rushed out the door. She grabbed the rusty rifle hanging on the wall and gave chase, screaming and banging the retreating Indian with the gun. Her husband decided she did not need help, as she had the upper hand. Later they found the Indian was a retarded one called Looney who lived nearby.

The earliest settlers had married Indian women and continued to live peaceably among their neighbors. Stockmen from the

Willamette Valley, seeking a drier climate for cattle and attracted to the rich bunch grass, had already lived among Indians. Children grew up with Indian children who became their friends. Yet, the Indians were unhappy at the encroachments on their former hunting and root grounds. Another change was in the making.

No Farther West

The Pacific Ocean.

As the nineteenth century drew to a close, the Indian problem was not yet settled. White people wanted the land, and the Indians were dissatisfied with their situation. Contact with the whites had changed the Indian's ways. Raiding parties and wars over horses were no longer practiced, but the Indians still had the same peculiar propensity for liquor that they had when they were first given it. Originally the excuse for giving alcohol was to increase their willingness to trade for furs. Later, the Indian was eager for liquor because it gave him the same exhilaration as a fast horse or racing car, until he drank himself into a stupor.

An Indian seems to have some different reactions than a white man. He thinks differently than a white man; whether due to his genes or his environment is for the experts to decide. He has a different feeling about the cultivation of the land, and for him there are no puritanical benefits in the exertion of work. Most Indians are truthful and have a sense of humor, yet they will swear to the truth of a fantastic tale when telling it to a gullible listener. They love to tell stories to those who will listen, and some of their humor is coarse. Bodily functions were called by the correct word, and one curious squaw was much surprised when a young childless white woman was resentful at being asked, "You know how to make kid?"

The Indians were sensitive. They were easily aggrieved at what they considered a slight, and if the wrong was not made right at once, it could become a monumental injustice that must be revenged. In adapting to white man's ways he found the clothing more comfortable, except moccasins, which he did not give up, the utensils more convenient, a gun more efficient, and a house more comfortable in cold weather.

The white man has changed, too. He has given up the idea of annihilating the Indians. He no longer looks at him as an animal; he has learned some tolerance and appreciation of another culture. While the white man continued to want more of the Indians' land, he thought of ways to secure it without bringing injury to the Indian. Not only had the white man changed in the West, but he became different than his Eastern brother.

Here the problem will have to be met, for there is no "Farther West" to which to push the Indians. In seeking an equitable solution it is best to remember what had been tried in the past.

When the first colonists came to America, they found the Indians friendly and helpful. The Puritans would not have survived the first winter without the help of the natives, who showed them how and where to fish, taught them what plants and herbs were edible or good for medicines, and shared with them their own meager supplies of corn. The newcomers needed help in getting to know what the country offered, and they needed kindness in that lonely wilderness. The Indians gave both.

The friendly natives helped protect them from hostiles to the north. It wasn't long before the town fathers were offering bounties for each enemy scalp that was brought in. This encouraged the habit of scalp taking.

The colonists also adopted the custom of using Indians for household tasks as well as heavy outdoor work. The Indians had used their own captives for such work, which now seemed to meet with the approval of the whites, but which was later disapproved of as slavery.

For nearly three hundred years, in their eagerness to build a nation superior to all others, our forefathers dealt with the Indians on the assumption that the Indians were a dying race. In time white folks came to realize that there was an Indian problem and later came to see it was indeed a problem when they wanted the same land the Indians claimed. To pay them, to drive them farther west, or to annihilate them were courses advocated by different whites.

When President Jackson assumed office, he felt great concern over what should be done with the Indians. He could see the fate of the tribes in the face of their imminent destruction. It was decided to send all the Indians west of the Mississippi to a section of land to be reserved for their use alone, where they would be able to work out their own advance toward civilization and where they would be protected from encroachment by incoming settlers.

The transfer of Eastern Indians to the West was provided in the Indian Removal Bill, the greatest question to come before Congress at that time. Involved was the massive transfer of the eastern Indians to land west of the Mississippi River to the plains considered unattractive to the whites.

By the end of Jackson's term of office every tribe east of Mississippi and south of Lake Michigan, save for two tiny bands in Ohio and Indiana, had come under the giant removal programs. Only a few thousand Indians were transferred from the Northeast, with the Iroquois ultimately resisting removal, along with a few in Florida, but 70,000 southern Indians were uprooted, and by 1844 only a few thousand, scattered in swamps and mountains, were left. The Indians were offered only the alternatives of removal or death. The five nations, Cherokee, Creeks, Seminole, Chickasaw, and Choctaws, refused to go willingly.

The first 4,000 Choctaws emigrated officially to their new lands in western Arkansas territory. Others followed that same winter, which happened to be an unusually severe one. They had left their warm homes lightly clad and had to struggle through the ice and snow of the Great Arkansas Swamp. To make matters worse was the lack of funds. Congress had appropriated money to pay the expenses which was to be disbursed through agents and contractors who agreed to take a certain number of emigrants into the Indian territory for so much money. Many of the contracts were given as political plums, as for instance the one given to a Major Francis W. Armstrong from President Jackson's home town of Nashville. He left Washington in November 1831 with $50,000 in his pocket to meet the expense of the first Choctaw removal, but the Choctaws were compelled to make the journey without funds, since Major Armstrong did not arrive with the money until February. He had spent the worst of the winter in his home in Nashville, because he had felt it was too cold to travel.

Removal continued for years. Experiences of this first winter which were bad later proved to have been the easiest of all. Cholera broke out on the trail over which the Indian exiles had to travel. Congress would not allow for any delays so the journey continued. It became known as "The Trail of Tears."

The Seminoles were transported from Florida around to the mouth of the Mississippi and Arkansas rivers in cheap boats, most of them rotten. When overloaded, they met the same fate as the Southeast Asians met in later years, when they became known as "Boat People" in their search for freedom.

The captured hostile Creeks were marched westward in double-file procession, manacled and chained together. The Cherokee, having resisted the longest, suffered the most in the process, as nearly one fourth of them died on the way.

Despite the promise given to these Indians that no part of this land would ever become a part of a state or territory and that it was to be designated as Indian Territory, in 1907 it became a part of the State of Oklahoma. The land was to be protected from white encroachment, a promise which fell before the overpowering demand of the whites for land. The promise could not be kept.

XXIII

Land Allotments

An Allotment House, built for the Indians to help them settle down to planting gardens and growing crops.

"Reservations" was the term applied to the idea of setting aside land for the Indian, where he would be expected to earn part of his livelihood, the rest being supplied by the Government. The treaties or settlements are all different, but in each case all Indians were to be encouraged to work their land, and to raise crops to supply their needs when the root and berry fields were confiscated and fenced by the incoming settlers. The amount to be paid for the land differed in each case.

Agents were set up at reservations and other places to administer the affairs of the Indians. They were appointed by the

President upon the recommendations of others or as political appointees. The President and Congress were far from the field of activity and had no real understanding of Indian needs, wants, or behavior. An agent's salary was $1,500 a year, and there were plenty of candidates as, unless he was scrupulous in his dealings, there was a good opportunity to better his finances to the detriment of the Indian. There was so much dishonesty and stupidity that the church interests brought the matter to the attention of the President. As a result the jurisdiction of each reservation was put in the hands of the various denominations to secure wise and honest agents, which is why the Yakima Reservation was given over to the Methodists with Reverend Wilbur in charge.

The reservation system was begun before the Civil War and bogged down during the conflict. But there is no doubt that the United States Government meant well when it promised the Indians their reservations with just compensation for the lands that the whites came to occupy. During the War between the States, funds for reservations were funneled into the Union's efforts to subdue the South. After the surrender came the Reconstruction Days and the great trek to the West.

The Indians were dissatisfied with trying to farm, and eventually the whites realized that this was not the answer to the Indian problem. Epidemics of disease continued to be destructive to the Indians, and many bands lost half of their people. The White Salmon band was reduced to twenty-one, and the Klickitats lost almost half.

In response to the problems, the Allotment Act of 1887 was conceived by Congress to break up Indian tenure and destroy tribal life in the belief that if an individual Indian were given a piece of land as his own, he would learn to use it for his benefit and have pride in it. There was little continuity to the regulations coming out of Washington, the agents continued to be interested in themselves, delivery of goods was sporadic, and communications continued to be slow. A change was needed, and to the white man the idea of Severalty Ownership sounded worth trying.

It required the Indian to fulfill certain regulations, just as the white man had to meet certain requirements in order to get a homestead. As a protection for the Indian, who was unaccustomed to financial dealings of that nature, the Indian's land was held in trust for a period of twenty-five years or longer, if necessary, which meant he could not lease or sell without the consent of the agent.

Quite a number of allotments in the vicinity of their former homes were taken by the Klickitats, who became friends of the whites settling amongst them. It was these Indians who have provided many of these stories that it is hoped will give a better understanding of life among the Klickitats.

When an Indian took an allotment, he had to go through just as much red tape as the white man taking a homestead, but he did have an agent who was to help him. In the Klickitat area the agent in Goldendale was Mr. Dunbar, who proved helpful to the local Indians. He saw to it that they got a house built, an orchard planted, grapes and berries planted, and were given plows and advice and encouragement on how to grow a garden.

By 1905, a total of 2,484 allotments had been issued. In 1914 when the rolls were closed, 440,000 acres had been alloted to 4,506 individuals; some sales to whites had been made from reservation land, where Indians still had jurisdiction of their acreage, but 700,000 acres of tribal property remained.

"No person who is not a recognized member of one of these bands (the fourteen original) or the child of such recognized member should be permitted to take an allotment."

Those who had allotments off the Yakima Reservation had the same rights on the reservations as those who lived on it.

XXIV

Wild Horses

Phantom.

The early Indians got most of their horses from trading and in wars, but in later times they came from the wild horse range in the Satus country. The folks out in the Glenwood area were interested in these horses as they had improved through the years, since men like Ben Snipes, known as the cattle king, had let his Hambletonian stallions run the range making a better breed of colts.

One of the Camas settlers by the name of Cody writes in a letter preserved by his sister, Kate, "In May 1906 we went to Logy Creek to buy wild horses. We bought 30 head, drove them home to the ranch, broke them to ride, then sold them at auction at a good price.

"Next year we went back in May to buy more horses, but we were too early so had to stay there for a week until the roundup started. We thought we would go down to Satus Creek where we knew some of the Indians, and stopped at Tune-washer's place, an Indian chief.

"Next day his wife went to Toppenish to get groceries and the Chief called us in the house to show us what he got during the war with the whites when they would come through the pass. He had two good sized trunks and unlocked one. The first thing was his large fur coat with a hood. He wanted me to put it on but I didn't want to as it had a peculiar smell. He kept at me until I put it on; he wanted to see how it looked. He pulled the hood (headdress) on my head and the feathers stood straight out in back and up over the hood. He seemed to be satisfied; I asked him if he used to wear it and he said, 'Yes, in war time.'

"Then next was a nice beaded vest; it showed him riding his horse, worked in beads on the front of it. It was magnificent, with gloves to match, and a beaded belt with a dagger and leather sheath. Next was about a dozen stone tomahawks with wooden handles; you could see the old blood dried on them. Then there were some old revolvers with hammers underneath, and a large pile of Indian money strung on buckskin strings.

"I saw a pile of hair but didn't give it a thought; the Indians made their rope of hair from the manes and tails of horses. I have seen them do it many times. I grabbed hold of it to see if there was anything under it and felt the dried hide. I took a look at it and saw that it was scalps; as near as I can guess there were about 35 or 40 scalps, mostly women—they had longer hair than a man. There were blonde, black, brown, and gray hair, all tangled up. He never said a word, just looked down. Not a word was spoken. My brother Guy just sat on the floor and looked. Then we picked up everything, put it back in the trunk and he locked it up. We looked for him to show us what was in the other trunk but he would not unlock it. We helped him put them away where he had them stored. He raised some short boards in the floor and put the trunks under the floor. He then told us not to tell anyone what we had seen and asked the blessing in Indian.

"The three of us walked out to our camp. We cooked dinner and he ate with us. We had known him for a few years. He was the manager of the roundup. Sometime between 1907 and 1908 his wife went to Yakima and when she returned she found him dead. Some of his patients had died and their relatives shot him. It is their religion."

On this range through the years were a number of outstanding horses, but one, especially, received much publicity in the Yakima papers. He was a beautiful golden stallion with flowing cream colored mane and tail. He had been sighted a number of times, standing atop some pinnacle of rock to keep guard for his band of mares. Many ruses were used to catch him in the roundup, but to no avail, and once when caught he escaped through the barricade when being driven into the corral. He was thought to be even more outstanding because of his spirited escape and became even more to be desired.

But at last he was captured and sold. None of the usual methods of taming could control him, to say nothing of riding him. Many wanted him, but no one knew what to do with the unquenchable spirit which drove him. The newspapers wrote stories of this beautiful horse, which they named "Phantom," because he had been elusive for so long before his capture. Reporters launched a campaign advocating his release, saying that he could never be trained and to try to do so would destroy him. The newspapers did a masterly job, and people wanted the horse released to his old haunts to build another herd of mares and thus improve the wild horse bands on the Satus.

A Yakima man was found who was willing to drive Phantom to Logy Creek. The effort was a little tempestuous, but it was successful. In going out of the corral gate the stallion gave it one vicious kick, and looking back at the clustered men, raised his head and gave one long neigh, much like the bugling of an elk, before bounding up the trail to freedom.

Through the years many of the young horses showed the markings of Phantom in color and spirit, and everyone, both red and white, felt great satisfaction in giving the horse his freedom.

However, ranges available to wild horses are becoming increasingly scarce. Even Indian reservations are being closed to the wild horses, the measurement of an Indian's wealth, because cattle raising is more profitable. Livestock management men have shown that two horses eat as much forage as three cows and graze closer to the grass roots. A cow, with fewer teeth, and utilizing longer-stemmed grasses is less destructive to the fragile prairie grasses. Partly for these reasons, Indian wealth was slowly transferred from horses to cattle.

Today's wild horses of the West are the offspring of many breeds through passing generations. They are so close to extinction that the Bureau of Land Management is thinking of setting up horse refuges.

The end of the wild horse range is coming for the same reason that the Indians are having problems. No one seems to know what to do with the wild horses or the Indians.

XXV

Food

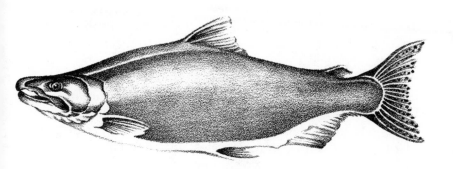

Salmon was a staple of the Indian diet.

From time immemorial, the Indians along the Columbia River have depended on salmon as their chief diet. They used to believe, and still do, that the salmon is a direct gift from the Creator just for them. He arranged it so the salmon would come in annual runs, the different kinds coming at different times from early spring to late fall, to relieve the winter shortage and give ample supply to prepare for winter storage.

The Indian and salmon have a peculiar relationship, and it is well to understand it better.

In the Columbia are four species of salmon. The Chinook has an average maturity of four years, although seven-year-olds have been taken. This is the king of all salmon and is often called Royal Chinook or Tyee, an Indian term for chief. They average about twenty pounds though one weighing 126 pounds and 6 ounces was caught at St. Petersburg, Alaska. They have bright skin, and red, firm flesh of superior quality. They are sea-going, or anadromous, fish, which lay their eggs in fresh water. They enter the Columbia in late winter or early spring and continue in the lower river for some time before heading up stream. In the spring it may take them two weeks or more to reach Bonneville, as if they knew that they had time to dawdle, but the fall fish travel much faster and have been known to reach the dam in ten days.

The Blueback and Chum weigh around four pounds, have a maturity of four years, and come later in the summer. The Blueback deposit their eggs in waters that rise in lakes. A well-informed ichthyologist can tell from which lake they came by the identifying markings on their scales, just as thumb prints identify a person. The Silver is a summer salmon that average eight pounds and mature in three years.

Because salmon do not eat after reaching fresh water, nature gives them extra supplies of fat and oil to carry them to their destination, which is the place where they were hatched. The best grade of salmon are the ones which have farthest to go to the upper reaches of the river. The Puget Sound Indians, with plenty of fish of their own, claim that the best salmon comes from the Mid-Columbia area. Bright salmon come up the Klickitat River in April and May.

Another unexplainable habit of the salmon after they enter the fresh water is that they tend to travel on the lee, or north, side of the river. This means when they come through the Cascades and up the Narrows, they swim on the most accessible side where the Indians can stand on the shore and get them with a spear or dip net.

The salmon is a fish of mystery. Ichthyologists have been able to learn about their life cycles, but they have not yet managed to discover how they are able to carry them out. No one can understand how they can detect the waters of the Columbia in the wide waters of the Pacific Ocean, and find their way up-river to the correct tributary that shields the gravel bar of their birthplace.

Having reached the destination, the female chooses a spot, digs a little depression with her tail, deposits her eggs, and moves away. The male then comes in to fertilize the eggs, covers them with gravel with a flip of his tail, and leaves. Both parents will die shortly and their disintegrating bodies remain in the water to nourish the young fry, which emerge in one to three months. They stay in fresh water as fingerlings from 1½ to 8 inches long and then migrate to the sea. It is a hazardous journey and many do not make it through the natural perils as well as the man-made obstacles such as power-generating plants.

On the upper Klickitat River is an old Indian trail crossing called Castile Crossing, where one can sit on the high grassy banks to watch the drama in the river below. The water is usually crystal clear, and it is humbling to see the drive that brought the fish for hundreds of miles to sacrifice their lives in this life process in order that the new generation might be born, with all this laid out in the river below as on a stage.

On the Klickitat River there is a salmon hatchery that uses spring water, which enters the hatching pond through a two-inch pipe just above the level of the pond's waters. When the salmon come up river to spawn and reach the pool, their drive is so strong that they mill about in an effort to enter the two inch pipe, much too small for their big bodies, but which has the waters of their birthplace.

Historians have estimated that, before the white man came to the Northwest, the Indians each year took eighteen million pounds of salmon from the Columbia. It once seemed as if the supply was inexhaustible. In the summer of 1883, forty-two million pounds were taken, the greatest catch of all times. Old settlers tell of fish so plentiful they could be harvested from small streams by being pitched out with a barnyard fork.

The white folks could not see such a resource at hand without putting it to some commercial use. The first commercial fishing business was started by Hudson's Bay Company vessels bringing trade goods to Vancouver and leaving with many tons of salted Columbia salmon packed in barrels.

In order to take bigger catches, the white folks helped the Indians build platforms on which they could stand out over fast water and get more fish. At Celilo the maze of platforms made a dramatic picture. In order to take bigger catches they used longer nets, and down the river they used teams of horses to pull in the huge catches.

The settlers were ingenious in developing better tackle and better methods. The fish wheel is said to have been worked out by some resourceful Scandinavians. The first wheel was built on the Columbia in 1878 by Samuel Wilson on the south side of Bradford Island where Bonneville Power House now stands.

A fish wheel was a large wheel or a double wheel, mounted on pilings or a scow, with scoops mounted between the wheels. Large quantities could be caught and dumped into boxes, where the fish were picked up by tenders. Fish canners prospered from this method until it was recognized that it had to be outlawed.

In provisions of the treaty of 1855, the right to take fish at Celilo Falls was secured to the Warm Springs and Yakimas, and this included Klickitats and Umatillas. The Nez Perce also claimed some rights. The language of the Yakima Treaty reads as follows:

"The exclusive right of taking fish in all streams, where running through or bordering on said Reservation, is further secured to said confederated tribes, as also the right of taking fish at all usual and accustomed places, in common with the citizens of the territory and of erecting buildings for curing them; together with the privilege of hunting, gathering roots and berries, and pasturing the cattle and horses upon open and unclaimed land."

Although the U. S. Government guaranteed the Indian tribes at The Dalles and Celilo the right to continue to fish there, they were expected to move onto the reservation set aside for them, where the Government endeavored to help them change from hunting to farming and stock raising with the hope that they would become self supporting. However, it is hard to get people to do what they do not want to do.

As might be expected, only a few moved to the reservations. Tradition remained too strong to allow them to leave their native haunts. Some of those who moved to the reservations soon tired of the restrictions placed upon them by the Indian agents. Some resisted the Christian religion, which was almost forced upon them. Their symbolic long hair was ordered cut by Congress in hopes of breaking their native habits, but the Indians were not used to being told what to do.

In later years, during the season closed to commercial fishing, at times the Indians were not supposed to sell their fish, and each year brought new rules trying to maintain good salmon runs. The whites made complaints about the Indians selling to canners and others. It was not uncommon to see an approaching white place a dollar bill under a rock and walk nonchalantly away, to return in a few minutes to find a nice bright salmon where his money had lain. Was there a double standard, or was the Indian supposed to adhere to the rule and the white man free to infringe?

The fishing site at Celilo became a tourist attraction in spite of the fact that one could smell it for some distance. It became a maze of scaffolds and platforms with cables to haul the fish from the rocky spots, while beneath them roared the tumbling white water of the falls. One reason fishing in white water is more successful is because the fish cannot see the nets. To catch a big fifty-pound salmon struggling in that fast water is a Herculean task. It was something to watch. It soon became mandatory for both the fisherman and the net to be tied to a secure post or rock.

Elation over large catches was always tempered by the thought of the hard work yet to be done. An Indian fisherman would fill a gunny sack with about seventy pounds of salmon and help his squaw, who was the burden bearer, to get it onto her back. After adjusting the weight properly, fixing the broad head-band which was stitched to the sack, and getting to her moccasined feet, she would shuffle off at a slow pace, never stopping until she reached her destination.

It was from the fall run of Chinook that the salmon were prepared for winter food. After the men caught the fish, the women cleaned and cut it in prescribed ways, then drying it on racks in the sun and wind, and sometimes smoking it near wood fires to hasten the process and keep the flies off. Only then was it pounded into meal for storage in grass baskets lined with roasted salmon skins, a method which preserves the salmon. No one knows how the Indians first discovered this method.

Other customary foods were roots and berries. West of the mountains the staple root was the wapato, a potato-like bulb found on Sauvie's Island and other such locations. They grew in lakes where the squaws dug them in four- or five-foot-deep water by clinging to their canoes and loosening the bulbs with their toes. The bulbs floated to the surface and were then thrown into the canoes. They were called Indian potatoes and since they did not grow east of the mountains, the Klickitats could only obtain them by trading.

For the Klickitats the principal root was the camas, a tulip-like bulb up to two or three inches in diameter which bears blue flowers on slender scapes. The camas was sometimes eaten raw, but was usually roasted and then prepared in various ways. A few of the older women still gather them, but the custom is fast dying out as the fields are fenced and food is easier to get from the grocery store.

The camas growing in damp meadows in early spring as a lovely blue flower was harvested in the summer after the stalks died down, a sign that the bulb had matured. When a field is in bloom, it looks like a beautiful lake of blue.

In digging the bulb, a digging stick of iron, about three feet long, curved and sharpened on the business end, having a "T" shaped handle, was pushed into the ground under the bulb, forcing it to the surface.

To roast these bulbs, a pit was dug, a fire built in it, and stones added. When all was heated to satisfaction, the remaining coals were raked out, the pit lined with the heated stones, leaves and grass placed on them, the bulbs dumped in, and more leaves and grass added. Then the hot coals and ashes were put in and all covered with earth. A twig about the size of a lead pencil was then pushed gently through the mound to the bulbs and very carefully removed, thus forming a vent hole. After 48 hours all was taken out, and the roasted camas bulbs were then ready for final preparation by being pounded into a doughy mass, shaped into cake-like patties, and baked. They have rather a sweet chestnut-like flavor, as described by white people who have not acquired a taste for Indian foods.

Another baked dish, but a sad substitute for camas, was prepared from the grey or greenish moss that is prevalent on the oak trees in some areas and was used in times of necessity, as a condiment mixed with wild onion, or as a filler with other foods. It took a lot of time and washing in its preparation, and tasted tarrish to those white folks who had the nerve to taste it.

The Indians also ate acorns and they were common because much of the Klickitat area had oak trees. The acorns have a considerable amount of tannic acid, they were boiled or roasted to make them edible. They were cracked, pounded into meal, and used as thickening for stews and in bread.

There were many other wild roots like wild onion that was the bane of the settlers as their butter was unsaleable when it took on an onion flavor from the wild onions eaten by the cows in the early spring pastures. The Indians used them liberally, especially in slightly tainted food.

In addition, there were wild carrots, wild parsley, wild celery, and many other roots grew in different parts of the fields and hills. Kouse was quite common and from it the Indians made what they called a "fist biscuit," because in molding it the squaw left her finger prints.

Many kinds of berries that grew on vines, bushes, and trees, were put to use as food, both fresh and dried. Of these the most important were the huckleberries that grew on the foothills of Mount Adams and elsewhere. Here there were great fields, from the lower elevations to high up towards timberline, that thrived well after forest fires had cleared out some of the bigger trees. This was the Indian vacation land, where they would go with the whole family and stay for several months.

Here there was good water, fuel, some game, a place for the children to play, room for the men to race their horses, and other men with whom to gamble. They would come up the trails on horses, riding single file with the babies in back boards and the older children hanging on wherever they could. They would come from all parts of the Mid-Columbia stopping at friendly settlers homes to trade for flour or other staples with the promise of returning later with baskets of huckleberries (and they never failed to deliver them). Most settlers gave them hay for their horses, because it was not too plentiful on part of the trail.

One rancher told an interesting tale of one such camp set up near his hay stacks. In the morning a buck came walking into their kitchen while they were eating their seven o'clock breakfast. He blurted out, "Where is my girl? You take her. Her tracks come to your gate." They all went to look and a little girl's barefoot tracks showed in the dust of the road coming to their gate. "You took her. You give back." The Indian's voice was threatening.

The settler asked, "What time did she leave camp?"

"Little moon up there," said the Indian, as he pointed to the southeastern sky. Just then they saw the little girl with her mother right behind, switching the little legs with a willow branch. They all went in to finish breakfast, and it took the rancher's family quite some time to figure out when the little girl had left the camp.

Many gallons of huckleberries were harvested each autumn. They were eaten raw, boiled, or mixed with other foods, but most of them were dried in the mountain sun or in the smoke from smoldering fires.

These mountain trips which would last for weeks or even several months, were regarded as vacations. The women gathered berries and squaw grass for baskets while enjoying the gossiping with other women, and they could watch the races and the stick and bone games. The men were avid gamblers and were sometimes unfortunate enough to lose all their possessions and even their wives. The Indians enjoyed socializing.

When the fall nights got too cold, they would load up their horses and start for their regular homes.

XXVI

Religion

The emblems of religion as practiced by the Shakers.

The Indians believed in an Almighty who had created the land for their use, providing it with fish, roots, and berries for their food. They believed in an afterlife which they called "The Happy Hunting Grounds," where everything was restored to health and perfection. They believed that every object was endowed with a Spirit.

In earlier times they practiced the Guardian Spirit Cult which required that a youth sought spiritual power by going out during adolescence on a long and lonely fast. Here he stayed without food or water, and while faint and semi-conscious, he was visited by a spirit which endowed him with power to be successful. He received a special talisman in the form of a song or dance to express his newly-given power.

The sun dance, seldom practiced in this Mid-Columbia region, was a dance to give a brave a certain status. This dance was one where the man was tied to a pole by thongs strung through the muscles of his breast. For three or four days and nights, without food or water, he would circle the pole, staring at the top of the pole as if it were the sun. He would become delirious and see visions brought on by the great pain of tearing himself free.

The Indians seemed to want to believe the missionaries, but it was an evanescent interest which wavered if they thought they were offered a better thing by another missionary. Even when they did accept the Christian faith, they expected a reward of food or clothing for attending services. It is doubtful that they had much real understanding of the doctrines, which were very different from anything they had known before.

A new religion sprang up in the Olympia area. To one of these small tribes was born John Slocum. In 1881, John Slocum, called Squ-sacht-un by the Yakimas and Klickitats, was "Unaccountably drawn to think of . . . the error of his ways and of the evil days that had fallen on his few remaining friends. Whiskey, gambling, idleness, and general vice had almost exterminated his people." He became sick and felt that he died, but was not allowed to enter heaven but he had a choice of going to hell or returning to earth to preach to the Indians. So his soul returned to earth and reentered his body; he began a crusade against whiskey, gambling, and "Boston" vices. With the help of his self-appointed high priest, Louis Yona Luch, he organized the Shaker Church, which practiced the highest morality, sobriety, and honesty. They used candles, bells, crucifixes, the paraphernalia of the Catholic, Presbyterian, and even some of the Indian religion.

A Shaker Church was built at The Dalles, which at one time in the late 19th century, had a large membership of ninety or more. The leader, Sam Williams, opened the church to anyone. The sign at the right side of the door read:

Indian Shaker Church
You are welcome. Please be orderly.
NO ROWDYISM ALLOWED
Minister

This sign is still preserved in the Winquatt Museum, and the church itself has been designated a historic place.

In 1905, Sam Williams went to the Lewis & Clark Exposition at Portland and came back with an Edison Gramaphone and a few records, which he played at the services. This, no doubt, helped the attendance. At a Shaker service there is a table to one side, or in an alcove, covered with a white scarf. Hand bells and a crucifix are set on the scarf and covered with a table cloth, generally blue or white.

The minister stands to one side of the table, and as the occasion arises, he reads from the Bible, chants and rings the bells. Which bell and how it is rung has some designated meaning in the worship, seemingly having roots in old Indian rituals in which drums and later bells, set the beat for the chant. In the chant, the person tells The Great Spirit of his desires and troubles. Candles were used for light, with the incandescent light seen as a symbol of the devil. A congregation was started in White Salmon, and in later years services were held at Klickitat by one of the Indian women who used a large array of silver bells. One can assume that the more bells, the more problems could be solved. The religion did much for the Indians, as it was a gathering place where some of the problems, like gambling and drinking, could be held in check, and the Indians thrive on fellowship.

Up on the Satus and in the neighboring villages where more of the Indians live, even today there are churches that conduct services that incorporate many of the old Indian rituals while in other respects belonging to either Catholic or Protestant faiths.

Myths and Legends

The legend of the "Bridge of the Gods" was known by many different Indian tribes in the Northwest.

It is from myths and legends that have come down by word of mouth by the Indian "story tellers" that one learns much of their beliefs. Because they had no written language, there were those Indians who remembered and retold these tales around a campfire, or wherever the opportunity arose. These same tales have been studied by ethnologists who can unravel the events to show some of the beliefs of the old timers. They can also tell of relationships between tribes by the way the story is told, or by the characters portrayed, even if they are called by different names.

Mr. C. O. Bunnell, who wrote the *Legends of the Klickitats*, grew up on his father's ranch on the hills above the Columbia, where the Maryhill Museum now stands, on the main Indian trail leading to Celilo Falls fishing grounds. There was a Klickitat camp, as well as a burying ground on their property, and there were many old paintings and carvings on the cliffs.

To get spending money he and his brother raised and sold melons and fruit to the passing Indians who traveled the trail. He related that the first complete tale he heard came from an old chief of the Shoshones, and it was a reasonable story of the Klickitat and Mid-Columbia Indians.

The legend of the Great Flood and the Origin of the Tribes was the Indian's conception of the flood, involving also the creation of the native tribes, and is one of the most fantastic native legends. This is the story of the great beaver, Wishpoosh, of Lake Kichelos. According to this myth, the beaver, Wishpoosh, inhabited that lake on the summit of the Cascade Mountains the source of the Yakima River.

"In the time of the Watetash (animal people) before the advent of men, the King Beaver, Wishpoosh, of enormous size and appetite was in the evil habit of seizing and devouring the lesser creatures and even the vegetation. So destructive did he become, that Speelyai, the Coyote God of the Mid-Columbia region, under took to check his rapacities.

"The struggle only made the monster more insatiable, and in his wrath he tore out the banks of the lake. The gathered floods swept down the canyon, and formed another great lake in the region now known as the Kittitas Valley.

"But this struggle between Wishpoosh and Speelyai did not end, and the former in his mad fury went on thrashing around in this greater lake. For a time the rocky barriers of the Umtanum restrained the flood, but at last they gave way before the onslaughts of the wrathful beaver, and the loosened waters swept on down and filled the great basin now occupied by the fruit and garden ranches of the Cowiche, Natches, and Atahnum. In like fashion the restraining wall at the gap just below Yakima City was torn out, and a yet greater lake was formed over all the space where we now see the level plains of the Simcoe and Toppenish. The next lake formed in the process covered the yet vaster region at the juncture of the Yakima, Snake, and Columbia River. For a long time it was dammed in by the Umatilla Highlands, but in the process of time it, too, was drained by the bursting of the rocky wall before the well-directed attacks of Wishpoosh. A yet greater lake, the greatest of all, now formed between the Umatilla on the east and the Cascade Mountains on the west. But even the towering walls of the Cascades gave way in time, and the accumulated floods poured on without hinderance to the open sea.

"Thus was the series of great lakes drained, the level valleys left, and the Great River able to flow in its present course. But there is a sequel to the story of the flood. For Wishpoosh being out in the ocean, laid about him with such fury that he devoured the fish and whales, and so threatened all creation that Speelyai perceived that the time had come to end it all. Transforming himself into a floating branch, he drifted to Wishpoosh and was swallowed. Once inside the monster the wily god resumed his proper size and power, and with his keen edged knife proceeded to cut the vitals of the belligerent beaver, until, at last all life ceased, and the huge carcass was cast up by the tide on Clatsop Beach, just south of the mouth of the Great River. And now what to do with the carcass? Speelyai solved the problem by cutting it up and made from its different parts the Indian tribes. From the head he made the Nez Perce, great in council and oratory. From the arms came the Cayuses, powerful with bow and war club. The Klickitats were the product of the legs, and they were the runners of the land, the belly was transformed into the gluttonous Chinooks. At last there was nothing left but an indiscriminate mass of hair and gore. This Speelyai buried up in the far distance to the east, and out of it sprang the Snake River Indians."

Another legend was of the Coming of Fire and the Tomanowas Bridge of the Gods.

Perhaps the most perfect and beautiful of all Indian fire myths is that connected with the famous "Tomanowas Bridge" at the Cascades. One legend, probably the best known of their stories, is to the effect that the downfall of the bridge, and the consequent damming of the river, was due to a battle between Mount Hood and Mount Adams in which Mount Hood hurled a rock at his antagonist, but the rock fell short of its mark and demolished the bridge instead.

"But the finer and less known version of the legend, which unites both the physical conformation of the Cascades, and the great snow mountains of Hood, Adams, and Saint Helens with the origin of fire, is to this effect: according to the Klickitats there was once a father and two sons, who came from the east down the Columbia, to the region in which The Dalles city is now located, and there the two sons soon quarreled as to who should possess the land. The father, to settle the dispute, shot two arrows, one to the north, and the other to the west. He told one son to find the arrow to the north, and the other to the west and there to settle and bring up their families. The first son going northward, over what was a beautiful plain, became the progenitor of the Klickitat tribe, while the other son was the founder of the great Multnomah nation in the Willamette Valley. To separate the two tribes more effectively, Sahale, the Great Spirit, reared the chain of the Cascades, though without any great peaks, and for a time all things went in harmony. But for convenience sake, Sahale had erected the great Tomanowas Bridge under which the waters of the Columbia flowed, and on this bridge he had stationed a witch woman called Loowit, who was to take charge of the fire. This was the only fire in the world. As time passed on, Loowit observed the deplorable condition of the Indians, destitute of fire and the conveniences it might bring. She, therefore, sought Sahale to allow her to bestow fire upon the Indians. Sahale, greatly pleased by the faithfulness and benevolence of Loowit, finally granted her request. The lot of the Indians was wonderfully improved by the acquisition of fire. They began to make better lodgings and clothes, had a variety of foods and implements, and, in short, were marvelously benefited by her bounteous gift.

"But Sahale, in order to show his appreciation of the care which Loowit had given the sacred fire, now determined to offer her any gift which she might desire as a reward. Accordingly, Loowit asked that she be transformed into a young and beautiful girl. This was effected, and now, as might have been suspected, all the Indian chiefs fell deeply in love with the beautiful guardian of the Tomanowas Bridge. Loowit paid little heed to any of them, until finally there came two chiefs, one from the north called Klickitat and one from the south called Wyeast. Loowit was uncertain which of these two she most desired and as a result, a bitter strife arose between the two. This waxed hotter and hotter, until with their respective warriors, they entered upon a desperate war. The land was ravaged, all their new comforts were marred, and misery and wretchedness ensued. Sahale repented that he had allowed Loowit to bestow fire upon the Indians, and determined to undo as far as he could, all the work he had done. Accordingly, he broke down the Tomanowas Bridge, which dammed up the river with an impassible reef, and put to death Loowit, Klickitat, and Wyeast. But in as much as they had been beautiful and noble in life, he determined to give them a fitting commemoration in death. Therefore, he reared over their bodies as monuments the great snow peaks. Over Loowit, what we now call Mount Saint Helens, over Wyeast the modern Mount Hood and over Klickitat, the grand dome now called Mt. Adams."

There were a number of men who became recognized as the story tellers and were called upon to tell the stories at feasts and gatherings. Among them was Ich-Pach-Pahl or Jim Looney, head of the White Swan Long House. Suntis Stahi was remembered but died long ago. Tia-a-Na-Ni was a religious dancer and drummer. Satus Jim Wagit, called Thomas Thomas Sam, lived at Wishram before The Dalles dam was completed in 1959.

Others were George Saluskin and his brother Jim, Chief George Meninick, directly descended from a treaty chief, and Sophia Wak Wak, granddaughter of Yakima Chief Kamiakin. There were many others, and while many whites enjoyed the tales, only a relative few recorded the stories.

XXVIII

The Underwood Families

A sample of the lovely bead-work produced by the Underwood women.

One must know their past history in order to get some understanding of the Indians, but to know them better, one must live near them and see their reactions to many experiences through the years. It is as George Gibbs says in his *Tribes of Western Washington*, "Of the externals of savage life on the Oregon Coast, there are many and full accounts; but an insight into their minds is not easy to reach, and those who have most carefully sought it are likely to be most doubtful of their success."

It is helpful to give some thought to the Underwood families, who lived near the mouth of the White Salmon River, after which the village of Underwood was named.

Amos Underwood came west as a young white man to seek his fortune. For a time he was engaged in running a flat boat in shipping wood to supply the river boats from various points to The Dalles. He served in the Volunteer Army and was present at the trial and execution at the Cascades in 1856, which left him feeling torn between the settlers and his Indian friends.

It must be recalled that after the Yakimas and Klickitats had escaped from the Cascade War, there was a strong feeling of revenge among the whites, and seven Cascade Indians were tried and found guilty. It was Amos to whom Chief Chenewuth had called out just before the hanging.

Shortly after the executions, one of the soldiers, Lieutenant Lear, bargained with Chenewuth's widow to buy her daughter as his bride for $250 in gold, but she cried, "No, no! You have killed her father, an innocent chief." However, other Indians were in favor of the marriage, which they felt would add to their safety from the warring Indians, and the mother was persuaded to accept.

The daughter, Taswatha, went to the tent of Lieutenant Lear and obeyed Indian laws after the mother had been given $250 in gold. He called her a new name, Ellen. They lived in the wife's village above the garrison, and Ellen made a good wife as she could cook, sew, and do bead work. Lieutenant Lear was devoted and kind for he was in love with the beautiful Indian girl. They got along well, and since they did not know each other's language, they learned to speak the Chinook jargon.

In time a girl was born to Ellen and Lieutenant Lear. She was named Isabella, after her father's mother in Virginia, and was a small dark haired girl, showing her French inheritance from the father's side of the family. Soon after the birth, Lieutenant Lear was transferred to Fort Dalles, where Ellen refused to go.

"All those strange white people," she said. "I could not live among them, or understand their language." So she went to stay with her mother while Lieutenant Lear went where the army sent him. He tried to see Ellen and Isabel, but wasn't permitted to do so as the divorce by Indian law was considered just as binding as the marriage.

Amos was given the young daughter at the time of execution, and when he saw her after a few years, he realized that he could love her. The other volunteers decided he would be lucky to get this lovely girl and so they were married June 1, 1857, after he had paid her mother, the bride price of $250.

In 1860, his brother, Ed, came to Oregon and lived with them. Amos spent much of his time working away from home, while Ed was a farmer. Amos sold their homestead for $191, which he considered a good price, and used his military land bounty to buy 320 acres at the mouth of White Salmon River. They built a fine log house with a wide porch across the front, barns, stables, and even a saloon, for Amos intended to have a business. They had a regular inn, and Ellen had to supply the meals. A school house was built for their children and a couple more from the neighborhood. He bought an iron stove for Ellen, which was her prized possession, because it had a reservoir for hot water.

When Isabella was eleven, Amos sent her to Vancouver to the Catholic school, where she could learn to be a lady and have the "Indian" taken out of her. When she returned the next spring, she got off the boat, and there she was, bustled and basqued like the pictures in the books.

Later Ed and Isabella decided to marry and had Reverend Condon of The Dalles perform the ceremony. Amos and Ellen had a ceremony performed at the same time, as Amos had heard that inheritance claims of an Indian wife were not always recognized among the whites. Amos and Ellen had three children, but only Mary grew to adulthood. Ed and Isabel built a house higher on the bluff and had ten children, three of them dying in infancy.

These Underwood women did much to arouse appreciation of Indian arts by having fairs in their home where they would persuade Indian women to display their handiwork.

Mary was married twice to white men but had no children, while Ed and Isabella had a large family. Year after year Grandmother Ellen would take each young child in turn to the viewpoint and tell them stories of the rocks, the weeds, and the birds and flowers. She worried about the attitude of these young people who were not interested in the stories, shunned Indian ways and language, and made fun of Indian names. They did not want their parents to speak anything but English. In this they were like the children of many other ethnic groups who cling to the language and ways of their old country much to the shame of their children.

These Underwood women taught the other Indian women how to do the intricate beadwork and basketry. They gave people an appreciation of the work and as a result, much has been preserved which would otherwise have been lost. Much can be seen in the Maryhill Museum.

Mary did not save only art work, for in addition she had acquired two of the medals given by Lewis and Clark, and she gave them along with other artifacts to the Maryhill Museum, all of which helped to give this museum its fine Indian Collection.

XXIX

The Wahkiacus Family

Sally Wahkiacus, a real friend to the whites and matriarch of her own people.

About fifteen miles up the Klickitat River from its confluence with the Columbia, the Wahkiacus family lived on the same allotment originally given to Sally ninety years earlier, which is still occupied by Cody, a grandson of the original allotment owner. They are the family for whom the crossroad store and post office are named. At one time it had been a railroad stop, marked by a signboard bearing the name Wahkiacus. The only other building was a little frame store with a built-in cubicle that served as a post office, and a lone gas pump which would supply gasoline in an occasional sale. Across the meadow and a short distance up the road stood a raw board frame house against a grove of pine trees, with a nearby orchard of fruit trees. This was the house that has been built on Sally's allotment. If one knew just where to look, one could glimpse, between the trunks of the pine trees, scattered head-boards that marked the graves of those family members who had gone before they could tell their stories to the white people who built the railroad or tended the store, the post office, or the lone gas pump.

Here and in the neighboring vicinity were allotments that had been assigned to other members of the Sally Wahkiacus family. These were days long before Equal Rights agitation, yet Sally was the unquestioned matriarch of the family. The Indian agent, Dunbar from Goldendale, had been helpful in setting up allotments for Sally, her father, Jim, and Frank, Joe, and Willie. The last three were Sally's sons, but no one knew who had been their father.

All the Wahkiacus family had allotments, and whether they were given special dispensation is not on record, but they all continued to live in the one small house that the agent arranged to have built on Sally's land. Mention has been made of other family members, but according to the old map, no land was assigned to them. James had made application #5 for an allotment of land, but this was the same piece of land claimed by Lewis C. Wright by right of pre-emption. On March 26, 1890, Mr. Wright filed declaratory statement #2547 with the U.S. Land Office for a pre-emption on the SE ¼ of Section 22, Twp. 4N, R L3E, and litigation ensued for more than twenty years.

On May 10, 1890, an Indian application #5 was made to the U.S. Land Office by James Wahkiacus; on December 30, 1891, he filed a relinquishment of allotment #5 with the Land Office, which James had no right to do, as these allotments were given in trust and no record for any such permission had been given by the commissioner. On January 17, 1892, the application was reinstated. On August 5, 1892, Pre-emption Cash Entry was made by Mr. Wright and receipt #4587 was issued to him for payment on a pre-emption of $1.25 an acre. On August 7 a patent was issued to James Wahkiacus by the Government, but he had never lived on it or used it.

It seems impossible that there could be so much confusion, which brought a lot of hardship to the new settlers. A possible explanation is that in those early days there was a shortage of trained clerical help; there were a number of bureaus involved, and there were changing rules. Mr. Wright had his receipt for the land and he had put up buildings and fences, whereas the Indian had done nothing but ride across it.

James Wahkiacus held an undisputed claim to the leadership of the Klickitats. He was the oldest Indian of the Klickitat Valley. He was no longer active, being crippled and bent nearly double with arthritis, but he was always eager to repeat his story to his neighbors of how he had "memaloosed" the whites when Kamiakin had led the Klickitats and the Yakimas in the attack at the Cascades in March 1856.

The Wrights had continued to have trouble gaining clear title to the land all those years. James Wahkiacus died in 1902, and finally, after taking the case to court, the Wrights were issued the patent for S.E. ¼ of Sec. 22, Twp. 4N, R L3E on January 15, 1912, twenty-two years after signing his first pre-emption papers.

How could these Indians, unacquainted with government ramifications understand? They felt the land had been theirs and still was even though it was given to the Wrights.

Sally Wahkiacus knew only a few words of English, but she knew Chinook jargon well, as well as her native tongue. She was eager to tell of the old ways and repeat stories handed down by her forebearers, until in her later years her deafness made conversation difficult.

To the first settlers she told repeatedly of the camp meetings held on the Columbia near Lyle and elsewhere. At that time the Methodist missionaries were still active at The Dalles, and she claimed to remember the building of the mission when she had been just a child. She remembered the hymn singing and even recalled some snatches of hymns and prayers, also describing the meals, which she called feasts. It is doubtful that she had been old enough to gain any real conception of the Christian religion, but she still had some belief at the time of her death, for she asked her friends, the Ludlums, to pray that she have a good watchman over her grave.

During the early years when there were a number of surveys over the Wahkiacus lands for railway rights, Sally received many promises but little financial benefit, and she grew suspicious. When McClellan came through on his way to Colville, he used the Klickitat pass, south of Mount Saint Helens and Mount Adams, through Peterson Prairie, Twin Buttes, and the huckleberry fields. He came over the Klickitat River, went up past Blockhouse, and on to Yakima with an entourage of 66 men and 173 horses and mules, such a band destroying all grazing for some time.

By the time the Columbia and Northern Railroad wanted access, she had learned to ask for a lifetime pass, and the use of it after the road was in gave her some of her greatest pleasures. After 1903 she frequently caught the train near her home and rode the red-upholstered seats for the twenty-odd miles to Goldendale. There she would meet her friends at the railroad station for a visit, where they sat on the platform, straight-legged, with their backs against the station wall. In an hour or more, she would return home with the train. The railroad crews got to know her well, and Conductor Goutcher was always kind to her. She remembered him with a couple of buckskin dolls as a gift.

Sally sometimes rode the train 15 miles in the opposite direction to Lyle to see Ellen Elkfoot, who was having trouble with the power company about land rights. Ellen had been visited by a man who wanted her to give up her land and who had given her gold coins to persuade her to do so, but when it came to signing the Skookum paper, they found she had no legal right to do so, for her land was held in trust and the land commissioner had not agreed to the deal. A short time later when the trust agreement expired, the agent again gave Ellen gold coins for water rights, but still she did not sign the paper. The power company brought suit, again it was brought out that she had no right to sign because, according to the old treaty, such rights had to be held for the benefit of the tribe. Ellen kept her gold pieces and the dam was built elsewhere.

The Indian women liked to visit their white neighbors as well, and Sally was very fond of Mrs. Harry Holmes at Klickitat. An added attraction was her new baby daughter, and often Sally showed up for little Nancy's bath. She would sit and watch the performance, rubbing the baby powder over the little white buttocks and back with her gnarled brown fingers. She would sniff the perfumed soap and finger the lovely soft baby clothes. One morning when Mrs. Holmes' sister, who was a guest from San Francisco and was making her morning coffee, turned from the stove to find an Indian right behind her. Startled, she screamed, dropped her coffee cup, and rushed to her sister, shouting, "There's an Indian in the kitchen!" Mrs. Holmes laughed and said, "Oh, that's Sally. She won't hurt you." Sally stayed for the bath ritual and her usual cup of coffee with coffee cake. She came often and always expected to go home with some little favor in the way of food or clothing.

When making such visits, Sally walked the railroad track. Eventually, several of the local men owned cars and, because there was no road, they were accustomed to drive on the railroad track. They usually gave Sally a ride, but they got tired of this practice and went on without her. But they did not pass her more than once. She figured out her own scheme and when she heard them coming, she lay down on the track, and lay there until they agreed she could ride.

Along about 1909 the settlers around Wahkiacus decided that they needed a bridge across the Klickitat River. The story of its building was told by Guy Long, who had come carrying his bag to a homestead on Wahkiacus Heights.

"To get a bridge, the homesteaders donated $1,700 in cash, besides work, and those who couldn't work gave cattle for sale to buy dynamite, nails, and stuff. Bill Moorhead had a span of mules, and he piled all the dirt up, and that's when Joe Wahkiacus got in trouble with the folks hired to build the bridge. Klickitat County was 'dry,' but Skamania County wasn't, so the bridge builders would go down to Skamania County on weekends and get whiskey and bring it back to hold them for the week. They began giving Joe whiskey and he kept wanting more. They didn't know what trouble they were getting into. They told Joe, 'No, you have had enough, you can't have any more.'

"So Joe got belligerent, and the builder hit him a lick and flattened Joe down. Joe went home to his house and got his 30-30. Joe was a good shot when he was sober. He loaded his gun but he was pretty drunk. He came over and climbed up on a pile of lumber, and Bill had his span of mules tied there. A fellow who had hurt his foot would come and watch and draw his wages, but when Joe began shooting, he could run better than anyone else. They all took up Swale Canyon to hide in the trees and brush to get away from the bullets, except one builder who stayed working, and Joe started shooting at him. The man ran up to Bill's father's place to get a gun to shoot Joe. He was told 'no' and that Joe would be sorry when he got over being drunk, and it was their fault for giving Joe whiskey. After a bit it quieted down and Joe was sorry. But no more whiskey for him."

When the train next came through on its way to Goldendale, Sally tried to climb aboard so she could go to Goldendale and report the incident to the Indian Agent there. The bridge builders held her, kicking and screaming, to keep her from going, which might have led to real trouble.

When Edgar Wright and Non Young were building the first little shelter on the Klickitat valley floor to stay in while herding their cattle, they were molested twice by a group of Indian bucks who came upon them unawares. Being unarmed they could only promise to go and see the Indian agent at Goldendale.

Mr. Langdon, of Walla Walla, invested money in the mineral springs located on the bank of the river, and he wanted to make a big venture out of it. Testing revealed that they needed to drill wells on the Wahkiacus land. As part of the recompense, they built Sally another house close to her old one. The family, which was growing after Frank married Mattie Slokish, a relative of the Slokish who was one of the signers of the treaty, slept in the one house with their rolls of blankets spread along the walls. At night the house became wall-to-wall bed rolls. The other house was used for eating and for working on skins, baskets, and bead work.

Their income was small and came mostly from leasing pastures, selling the handwork done by the women, and selling salmon to the canneries or the white settlers. The men who could have worked at the nearby sawmill, chose not to as they found the work too confining.

When they sold a horse to their neighbor, Albin Berglund, the menfolk stood around to watch the fun, for they expected Berglund to be thrown when he tried to mount the horse, which, accustomed to the ways and smells of the Indian was expected to resist being handled by a white person. However, Berglund paid for the horse, jumped on it bareback, and trotted out to the road without incident. The disappointed men could not understand it.

Another time Mr. Berglund was putting up a better fence for his pasture. Joe, who saw this and resented such action on what he considered to be his fence line, came storming over to Berglund to stop him. Berglund, calmly putting staples in the post to hold the taut wire, straightened up as Joe started haranguing, and said, "Joe, you are drunk. You better go home and sleep. Come and talk to me when you are sober." Joe saw the hammer held prominently in Berglund's hand and went home.

Sally was a good friend of Hazel Vause, who had the store and post office in Wahkiacus. She would come to Hazel for any advice she needed about any reservation business, and she would borrow money from Hazel when in need. Hazel took her to Portland on business, where she and Sally enjoyed being the center of attraction when curious people gathered around them. Hazel took her to Warm Springs, too, where she had many friends. She trusted Hazel and would do whatever Hazel said.

One time, however, she did get mad at Hazel, and she had a sharp tongue, even though the tongue lashing could not be understood. At the time of the complete eclipse of the sun, in 1918, the white people knew what was happening but they had not thought to tell Sally. As the sun was obscured and the day darkened Sally became frightened and thought the end of the world was approaching. She and her family began chanting and singing, with frantic drumming and dancing. As it got completely dark, the wailing could be heard even by distant neighbors. Regular chaos ensued and to their way of thinking, they must have been heard by the Great Spirit, for daylight came back and the world was spared. When she learned the truth, she got mad at Hazel but later was embarrassed over her emotional outbreak.

In her later years she became quite feeble and walked with a cane, and she became hard of hearing. One day she was approaching the crossing of the railroad track at Klickitat and it was almost time for the train to come. She walked along down the track, lost in her own thoughts. There was a new engineer on duty and he saw Sally toddling along on her moccasined feet. He blew the whistle, but she made no response. He whistled loud and long, but she made no move to get off the track. He applied the brakes, but it wasn't soon enough and she was knocked down and shoved a few feet along the gravel.

Poor Sally had not heard. They insisted on bringing her to the hospital, but she just screamed for them to get Hazel, who came and assured her that she should let them take her to the hospital, which was in the charge of Dr. Gale and his wife Betty. Fortunately, there were no broken bones. Her bruises were attended to, and she was put into a nice clean bed. She quieted down and a little later when Betty Gale went in to check, she found no patient. Sally, unable to be comfortable in the high hospital bed, had crawled out and lain down on the floor between the bed and the wall. She lay on the floor during the rest of her hospital stay, but appreciated the luxury of back rubs.

Frank, her son, had married a Yakima girl, a member of the Slokish family, descended from a signer of the treaty in 1855. She was Mattie and a fine person and became the mother of a nice family of seven children. They lived in a modified Indian style, the only new element being that the children went to school in the one-room school house up on Wahkiacus Heights. Several of them did well, but didn't continue. One of them, Cody, was one of the boys serving in the U. S. Armed Forces during World War II, and when he returned, his family got together and went through the Indian ceremony of giving him a new name, that of Slokish, his famous relative, in honor of his service. Cody still lives on his grandmother's allotment.

Mrs. Ruth Toomey, who lived in Klickitat, became very much interested in Indian history and got to know Sally well. In October, 1930, she went to see Sally but could not find her, and the house was empty. After a search she found her in the Sweat House, where she had gone for treatment.

For the Indians the Sweat House has been used since the beginning of time. The Sweat House was part of their tradition, not only as a method of cleaning themselves, but also as a way to restore their health and renew their spirits. The teachings about the practice vary from place to place and family to family.

The Klickitat Indians built their sweat houses from willows or other limber branches bent into a dome shape and tied in place. This dome was covered with tule mats, or skins, with a crawl-through door facing the east. The floor was usually covered with pine or fir boughs which gave off a pleasant odor. Rocks were placed on the right side of the hut after being thoroughly heated in an early fire, as sweat baths were always taken in the morning. After entering, one pulled the mat over the door opening and poured cold water over the hot rocks. All this was done with prayers to the Great Spirit, staying as long as there were burdensome thoughts, sadness, or illness. The final act was a plunge into cold water, preferably a running stream.

Men and women did not use the sweat houses together, the women bathing after the men and boys had finished.

Sally had come here for treatment, but the stones were now cold and an east wind had chilled the Sweat House until Sally was too stiff to move. She had not been able to get up and go to the house, so Mrs. Toomey helped her home, made a fire in the cold stove, and gave her hot tea, for which Sally was touchingly grateful. When she died at Christmas time that year, Frank went to the sawmill to buy boards for her coffin. When asked what size boards, he wanted to go to the lumber shed and pick them out. He did not know how to describe the sizes he needed but would stand against the board and measure by the width of his shoulders. Sally was buried in the family cemetery which had held the other members of her family for no one knows how long.

For the most part life settled down quite peaceably in the valley, with an exception being some trouble over the Wrights' land. One of the Wright daughters told the story of the difficulty in this way.

"My father fenced in his land, and the old Indian trail went through it, so he built a gate at either end of the trail, and while they still used the trail to go through the place, they would not shut the gates. It was too much trouble. Of course, the stock would get out, and the stock roaming the hills would get in. My father kept asking them to close the gates, but they wouldn't do it, so he just nailed them shut and made a trail around the fence. Because that made the trail a little longer for them, the Indians grew very angry, and they came one day when just my brother, Edgar, was home. They threatened him and wanted to fight.

"These were the Wahkiacus Indians, and the Skookum was with them too. Later, my brother was clearing a piece of land, working some distance from the house. He carried a pistol as he was afraid; the Indians were acting ugly and kept tearing down the fence. He continued to carry the pistol as he thought that would help him protect himself, if a lot of them came and jumped him.

"So it went on. Finally, one day they all came to the house, but my father was home. My brother joined my father when he saw all the Indians arrive. One of the Indians named Jim Hunt, who had married into the Wahkiacus family, had his wife with him. He said her horse fell with her, going around the rocky trial and hurt her. 'Well,' my dad said, 'If you'd shut the gates, I'd be glad to let you through the fields, but you won't do it, and I built that trail for you and I want you to use it.'

"As my father said this, he motioned with his arm, and as he did so, he struck an Indian across the face. One of the Indians, Joe Wahkiacus, ran and grabbed my brother around the waist and my brother had the pistol in his back pocket and was trying to get it out. In the scuffle the gun went off and the bullet grazed the Indian across the forehead. This subdued them and they went up to Goldendale and Skookum went along with them, as he did their interpreting. The Indians claimed they had been shot at six times, and Joe had smeared his wound with huckleberry juice to make it look real bloody. Mr. Van Vactor was the sheriff and he came down and took my father to jail."

It happened that the night Mr. Wright was put in jail, a few of the Glenwood settlers were in town to get their winter's supply of flour and staples, and when they heard about the trouble, they paid his bail, and he was fined $20.

Tragedy came often to the Klickitat Indians. One morning one of Sally's little granddaughters, while playing in the yard, was bitten in the hand by a rattlesnake. As far as is known, no medicine man was called, but Frank and the family tried whatever Indian cures they knew but with no benefit. At noon they decided to go to the village where there was a small mill hospital and doctor. Perhaps, it had been already too late for anti-venom, and there was some difficulty in obtaining it. At any rate, little Wanda died.

Funerals were important ceremonies among the Indians. Friends and relatives come to join in the wailing and chanting, bell ringing, and drumming. Their prolonged mourning gave an eerie feeling to the rituals. Elaborate feasts were served after fresh deer and salmon had been secured, with additional food brought by friends, both whites and Indians. All this while the corpse lay in state after a service where the body was dressed in the best clothes and blankets. After the casket was removed to the burial plot, the whole house was brushed with wild rose branches and the floor scrubbed to get rid of evil spirits. To be sure that Wanda, whose white father was no longer around but had been chased away before her birth, had a proper send-off the white neighbors were invited in to conduct an extra service of white man's prayers and hymns.

Funerals were a financial drain on the family finances, because generous food must be supplied, even if the money had to be borrowed for purchases from the local store.

Another story tells of Joe who had been drinking heavily and on his way home from The Dalles lay down on the railway track for a little rest. He fell asleep, failed to hear the oncoming freight, and was killed by the train. Whether true or not, an Indian of today when asked about it, just shrugs his shoulders and gives the stock answer, "It was too long ago."

Jim Hunt, Sr., was another old Klickitat who lived on an allotment in the White Salmon Valley had been one of the party of attackers at the Cascades, but he always refused to talk about it. When he died in 1902, he was more than 100 years old. He became a sort of curiosity to the settlers, and many tales grew up about him. Each day he would ride down to the village of White Salmon to visit with any friend who might be about. He got some money from leases and small tribal payments, but he always expressed his fear of losing it if he put it in the bank. Instead, he told that he buried it on his land.

This was of much interest, to one son especially, who tried to get his father to tell where the money was hidden, so as to be able to find it in case the old man got sick.

But Jim was a wily old man and no one found out. When he did sicken and die, his son hurried home so as to start digging before anyone else could do so, but even with the help of metal detectors, neither the son nor anyone else ever found the money. It is one of those stories that add interest in a community.

One of Frank and Mattie's daughters, Inez, married Andrew Jackson and continued to live at the old home. She and her husband had a family of nice-looking and alert children, who attended the local school.

Inez became a member of the Shaker religion. She, herself, became a leader and had services in her own home, no doubt hoping that by this faith she could protect her family from the use of alcohol. It was surprising to come to her house with broken-down cars standing about in the yard and enter from the decrepit stoop to find a nicely-paneled and vinyl-floored room with a white covered table against one wall on which were the silver bells and cross that Inez used in her Shaker services. Here too tragedy struck, and one of her sons was killed.

Frank Wahkiacus, when he grew to be an old man and was not in very good condition, did not feel able to accompany his family when they all went to The Dalles. On their return from one such trip, his grandson Eliot ran into the house to see how Frank was and found him stretched out on the floor. They suspected evil play but found that he was clutching a bottle marked, "poison, wood alcohol." Frank couldn't read.

Now Frank rests with Mattie, Sally, Jim, and those other family members who loved this Klickitat Valley and were even fond of the white folks who had come to live among them. He was mild mannered and kindly. He continued a line of friendly

Indians who have become interested in preserving some of the old arts of basketry and beadwork. One, especially, who has promoted these crafts is Nettie Kuneki, working in White Salmon as Mid-Columbia Council chairman.

They had been friendly to the whites, but, when looking back, it seems that the same white neighbors should have been more helpful in both church and school.

XXX

The Spino Family

Louise, a happy personality and friend to all in trouble or need.

Another family that was well known in the Klickitat Valley was the Spino group. Here we find that it was the woman who became the head of the family, and everyone knew her as Indian Louise. She was a friendly out-going person who spoke better English than most.

Louise, a gregarious person, loved to tell stories of the olden days, to laugh at her own jokes, and to befriend any neglected child among her relatives or friends. During the depression years of the 1930's she called on a regular route of friends whom she visited in hopes of some little help in the way of food or clothing, offering in return the first chance to buy a fresh salmon or steelhead. She was a good story teller and gave to her stories a little of the flavor of the Indian point of view. She regretted that she could not read or write and was determined that her children would not be so handicapped. She was determined that her children were not going to be "dumb Indians."

Some of the stories she liked to tell were about her forebearers. Her grandfather on her father's side was Ben Van Pelt, a French Canadian who had come on a river boat from the Snake River to Celilo. Louise remembered him as a handsome man, but what she remembered best were the brass buttoned jacket and the visored cap all decorated with "gold" trimmings of a river boat pilot. His wife, Susie, who was Louise's grandmother, was a full-blooded Indian maiden of the Celilo tribe.

Besides being a river pilot, he owned a saloon at Columbus, which is now known as Maryhill. The man who ran the saloon for Ben knew where he kept his money hidden, so he killed Ben to get the money. Ben was buried at Columbus and left a widow and two children, the older of whom was William Van Pelt, Louise's father.

Louise liked to tell her story and it is given here in her own words.

"My other grandfather was John Tiawanous and he used to live at Spearfish, the place called Wishram, and the Indians called it Wishlam because they had no "R" in their language. Before he got an allotment in Section 26, he never stayed home, and he herded sheep for others. My grandmother's name was Susie, too, so both my grandmothers were named Susie. I guess that name is easy for the Indians to say, for there were many Susies. They belonged to the Wasco tribe at Spearfish, where they lived before they came to High Prairie. My grandfather fished in the spring and then he herded sheep for Leo Bruin, a sheep rancher on the Columbia."

Susie and John Tiawanous had five children: Dave, Matt, Harry, Mary, and Nellie. All of the children grew up loving whiskey, with the exception of Mary, and they all met violent deaths. In a drunken brawl Harry hit Matt over the head with a rock and killed him. Harry lay down on the railroad track one day for a rest, went to sleep, and the train came along and killed him. Dave injured his leg in some way, went to a doctor, was given wood alcohol to rub on his leg, but he thought it smelled like whiskey, tasted it, found it to his liking and drank it. Naturally, it killed him. Next, the grandfather met a tragic end as best told in Louise's words.

"I was born on High Prairie, December 8, 1897. My maiden name was Louise Van Pelt, my father's name was William Van Pelt and my mother's name was Nellie Tiawanous. They moved to High Prairie when he married my mother. My grandpa owned the property, but he never stayed home so my father moved there so he could care for us. My father and mother had both been married before, and when she married my father at The Dalles, her name was Nellie Snutups. This first husband had been wished dead by an Indian doctor. William Van Pelt was also previously married, and his first wife died in childbirth. Two children were born to this union and one died but the one girl, Isabel, is still living. My parents had horses, cows, and grain. Our house was an old shack-like one-room house. Me and my dad and mother lived in the house, and George and my grandpa and grandma did too." It seems George was a distant relative, a crippled boy who was raised by the family. He was born crippled and his parents wanted to kill him, but the grandma pleaded so hard for his life that they gave him to her.

"One day my Grandmother Susie, my mother, and I had been to Toppenish. On the way home we were camping at Bressie Springs on the reservation when a coyote howled five times. Grandmother knew he was trying to tell us something, but she couldn't make it out. Also an owl came to camp and hooted three times, but she still could not tell what he was trying to tell us. When we got home, Grandfather was not there but his black horse was. When my father came, he took the black horse and went to search and found where my grandfather had been thrown over a steep cliff. He had lain there for five days after his horse had thrown him. My father brought him home but he lived only two days."

William and Nellie continued to live on the homestead, and two girls were born to these two, Louise and the one who died without a name. They were the only children Louise could remember. Four years after the death of John Tiawanous, his wife died. She was believed wished dead by an Indian doctor and she was buried on the Memoloose Island near Spearfish, later being moved to the High Prairie Cemetery, which was called Hartland at the time. Fourteen of Louise's relatives were moved from the island because of the coming high water from The Dalles Dam. Many more have joined the earlier ones.

Louise explained that to wish a person dead, the Indian doctor (unknown to them) shouts the spirit of death into whatever the person happens to be eating. The food being eaten at the time causes your death, and the food never digests but returns from the body the same as when eaten. The possession of the spirit of death can be passed down from generation to generation unless it is killed. This Indian doctor with the spirit can be killed in two ways. One, by being murdered by the dead one's father or son, and the other way, by the person holding (unknown except by him or her) an object in his hands and having a person cut with a sharp knife between the closed hands. The object that is cut is then thrown into the fire.

Louise's mother, Nellie, used to work for one of the settler's wives, Mrs. Rollin Stearns, doing the washing and helping with the housework. Louise's father was a fairly good carpenter and built excellent fencing in straight lines, of which he was truly proud. Mr. Stearns had him clear the fields of rocks and use them to construct fences dividing the ranch's pasture plots. Since this was demeaning work for an Indian buck, he found a few squaws to do the work for him while he superintended the job. They did a good job and the dividing lines which are still there have been a source of conjecture by tourists.

Mrs. Stearns reported Louise's parents as being "agreeable workers" except they liked whiskey as most of the Indians did. They also liked the white man's food which was another inducement to work for the whites.

Many of the white women in the area hired Indian women to wash for them as washing sheets on a washboard and wringing by hand was hard work. The Indians did not hesitate to take time off for a trip to The Dalles, and Fred Smith, who lived on the

Columbia, told of William and Nellie more than once staggering home through his yard trying to reach the shelter of his barn, where after sleeping it off, they sheepishly went on home.

For a number of years the Van Pelts made their own moonshine unmolested by the authorities, as their place was hard to get to. When he was seen riding his black stallion on the canyon rim above the river across from the little sawmill town of Klickitat, everyone knew some lumberjack had made a purchase and would cross the foot log over the river to collect his booty, hidden near a specified tree stump. He had to be careful not to sample too much of the potent liquor or he would have to "coon" the bridge on his homeward way. The problem for the Van Pelts was that they liked their own product too well and would celebrate for days until the moonshine was gone and they would have to sober up enough to start another batch. One time they overdid their drinking and got into a fight and shot and killed each other. Although there were no witnesses, the authorities who were sent to investigate came to that conclusion.

When Louise was about seventeen, she married Joseph Sconowah. They had five children and lived on the allotment on the High Prairie on the breaks of the hills just above Klickitat. The children went to the Wahkiacus school on horseback. Joseph Sconowah died on Memorial Day after being "wished dead." Again, Louise felt that an evil spirit had taken a member of her family.

Later she married Roy Spino, a Klickitat Indian, and in 1940 they moved to their new home at Wahkiacus, which was an abandoned school house that they had bought from the school district. Louise was determined that her children should learn to read and write, because she always regretted that she had never gone to school. It is incongruous that she should have felt so strongly about her children going to school when she, herself, harbored such old beliefs as being "wished dead." To see that her children attended regularly, the Spinos bought an old car and drove it to school, using it as the family school bus. At least, attendance was as regular as the old car would permit.

Roy and Louise had ten children. Death took two of the girls. Ellen, the oldest daughter, was a lovely Indian maiden who answered the description of the romance writers. She wore a beautiful white buckskin suit and rode a fine bay horse, and she knew that she attracted admiring attention. She married a Warm Springs Indian but lived in the Klickitat area as her descendants still do. She met a tragic death under suspicious circumstances although the subsequent hearings resulted in no prosecutions. Louise was very fond of her family and grieved over the loss of Ellen.

Louise was always interested in school and community affairs. One of the things she enjoyed was to give programs for the women's clubs around the county explaining the preparation of Indian foods. She prepared foods made from local roots and berries, with samples for those women venturesome enough to taste the unusual foods. They found camas of especially good flavor. All these roots and berries, together with game and salmon, made a varied diet for the native.

She always attended school sports events even if she had to bring some young grandchild in a cradleboard or "te-ca" board. She was proud of her good-looking grandchildren and enjoyed it when the white folks admired the black-eyed little ones.

Louise used to tell about the work that Kamiakin did among the tribes in gathering food and ammunition for the wars that he was planning when they hoped to eradicate the whites. She told how each family was urged to lay in extra supplies and store them in caves along the Little Klickitat. Kamiakin bragged that he had supplies for three years of war, but they were never all used.

She also told of one village near Goldendale where women, children, and old men were wiped out in a massacre while the warriors were out on a raiding expedition. Indians were sometimes as ruthless and cruel to their own race as they were to whites.

Roy, her husband, fished and worked off and on at the sawmill. Their sons could become quarrelsome, especially after having some liquor. One day at noon in 1945 after listening to their bickering, Roy got up from the table, went across the room, picked up his gun, and shot himself. In telling of this, Louise only said, "I guess he got tired of living."

The young people of Louise's family have scattered, but one descendant, Doreen Mahaffy, is left in Klickitat doing fine work in trying to maintain some of the old culture, raising a family, and working as a teacher's aide and as a Sunday School Teacher.

It is true Louise never went to school and could not read or write, but from six years old she must have had an intensive training from her mother and grandmother. Before the age of six, a typical Indian child's life was full of love and affection; with no duties or tasks to do. They were not punished and received constant attention. But at about the age of six, girls began to learn the household duties. The tasks were many. They were taught how to prepare meats and fish, how to store them for winter use; how to dig and prepare roots, and how to harvest wild berries and dry and preserve them. There were skins of game to tan and prepare for use in moccasins, clothing and blankets. They had to learn how to make the grass baskets and the imbricated ones that became known as "Klickitat" baskets. The tasks were endless and Louise was proficient in all of them.

It was the boys' duty to learn to be good hunters and trackers, to be brave warriors, and to be shrewd traders. Louise's boys were not interested in farming but fished whenever they could during open seasons. They sometimes made money faster than they knew how to use it properly. Since alcohol was such an attraction, observers have often wondered whether the Indian Agency should have been more concerned about Indians living on outlying allotments off the reservation and more helpful to them in adjusting to the white man's civilization.

XXXI

Skookum Wallahee

Skookum Wallahee, a Klickitat chief.

Just down the road from the sawmill town was where Skookum Wallahee lived on his allotment. He had been chosen the chief of the Klickitats after Jim Wahkiacus' death. It was here that the Indian Agent, Dunbar, had helped him select the land that was to be his if he lived up to the requirements of the Allotment Act of 1887. The government had built a frame house on a small knoll, planted an orchard of apple, cherry, and plum trees, and set out a few grape vines on the sunny slope not far from the house.

There was an open meadow down toward the river where he could plant a garden and small grain field. The hills offered grazing for his ponies. The only access to the outside world was the Indian trail that ran along the river, and any necessary hauling had to be on a "take off" from the Lyle-Glenwood road up on the plateau, and down over the breaks, and through the trees.

The earliest settlers believed that Skookum was a brother of Sally Wahkiacus, but this is one of the mysteries of Indian relationship that never got settled. Skookum, himself, called Jim Wahkiacus his "pappy" and insisted he had always lived in this valley.

He used to tell that the remains of the winter homes at the mouth of the Little Klickitat where it joins the Klickitat River were those of his people. Here they spent the cold winter months. All that remain to be seen today are the now empty pits about twelve to sixteen feet across that still have the charcoal and ashes in the central fire spots. They originally had been several feet deep and covered with domed branches, mats, and dirt, with but one access opening. Some things about these early Indian neighbors could only be surmised, as they were not communicative until they knew you well and came to like and trust you. Even then, they could maintain a stony silence if they felt that you were prying, and look at you as if you were not there.

Skookum had been given a plow and a harness for a team, so with advice he had planted a garden, and its virgin soil and location produced luscious strawberries and sweet watermelons. In the years when the railroad surveying and grading crews came through, they were always anxious to get some of Skookum's berries and fruit. His neighbors, too, were good customers, and he was always eager to make a sale. The only time he would give away fruit such as apples was if he were promised an apple pie in return. He had a regular route that he followed to garner apple pies, and his capacity was limitless. He learned in off season that even dried apple pies were good.

Skookum had two squaws, an older one from the reservation country and a younger one from Lyle. They were hardly ever with him at the same time. When one would leave, he would go to get the other, and often paid her with a pony to persuade her to come back. The older one was reserved and would not visit the whites, while the younger one was talkative and friendly.

He had several children who all died from disease or accident. Stories were told that he had several children and wives as a young man, but of this he never talked.

It is fortunate that the settlers who knew the Indians can tell us what they were like, as it is from these reminiscences that one gets a better knowledge of the Klickitats. It is of such memories better understanding comes and will be of help in solving the Indian problem.

There had never been any serious trouble with the white neighbors except the one instance when a group of Indians had accosted the Wright family about the gates that had been made across the trail. The field in the Wright homestead had been fenced to keep the cattle in and when the Indians used the trail, they found it too much trouble to close the gates, and so the cattle would get out or the range cattle would come in. It was during this fracas that Mr. Wright was taken into custody and fined $20 and the Indians admonished to use the trail Mr. Wright had provided and to stay out of his fields. During the commotion Skookum was grappling with Mr. Wright and Mrs. Wright grabbed a nearby flower pot and gave Skookum a sock across the back. She was frightened that she would be in trouble, but Skookum had been so excited that he had not even noticed. This was really a fight with the Wahkiacus Indians and Skookum was merely the interpreter.

Skookum knew English quite well. When a young man, he spent much time at the James O. Lyle home at Lyle to be with their young son, George. Here he learned English, which was unusual for an Indian, who were usually satisfied to learn a little jargon.

These Klickitat Indians had ancestral fishing rights on the Columbia River, and most of the fishing was done along the Narrows, before the white people showed the Indians how to build scaffolds and trolleys over the falls so they could fish at Celilo. The Klickitat Gorge was also a good fishing place.

To augment his finances, Skookum sometimes loaded his wagon with fish and traveled into the Pannakinic and Glenwood areas where the settlers were often happy to buy fish. On these trips he would always go past the one-room school house, not to sell fish, but to give the youngsters a thrill. He would creep up to the windows, rise up, make awful faces, wave a tomahawk, and give out an awful yell. He got a thrill out of seeing the children rush up to the teacher, who was usually not much older than they, and try to hide behind her. He would finally go inside, smiling and friendly, but the children did not quite trust him. Older folks who grew up in those times tell how the mothers used Skookum as a threat when the children disobeyed.

It had been hoped that Skookum would cultivate all of his land, but outside of a garden and sometimes a small field of grain, he found it more to his liking to lease the land to the settlers.

When Rollin Stearns first settled on the river, he hired Skookum and Joe Wahkiacus to clear an acre of land for $25 and their dinner, as long as the job lasted. Rollin had not yet learned the way of the Indians for they would come to work in the morning shortly before noon and leave early in the afternoon, making the work last a long time, because they liked to be fed the white man's noon-time meals.

Stearns rented Skookum's place for a number of years, and whenever Skookum wanted advice, he would come to see the Stearns family. He even let Mrs. Stearns photograph him, and when he found that it did him no harm, he was willing to have his picture taken many times.

In the early 1900's there had been much interest in building a railroad along the Klickitat River from Lyle to Goldendale as an outlet for agricultural products. This called for more surveys through the Indian allotments with surveying crews and observers. There had been some railroad agitation ever since McClellan had gone through the country in the 1850's, and the local Indians were tired of the visits. The route was planned to go through both Skookum's and Sally Wahkiacus' properties. One survey went right through Skookum's pole barn. Finally, a financial settlement was accepted by Skookum, but payment was slow in coming, and to expedite this matter, Skookum would sit on the hillside above the working crews and roll rocks down onto them. It was a delicate situation, as they had to have his good will. With payment, a life pass on the railroad, and a new pole barn, peace was restored.

After the railroad was completed, it was Skookum's delight to catch the train anywhere along the line, as that is what the pass allowed. He would take the daily train to Goldendale, visit his friends, and return in the afternoon. He would stroke the red upholstery as he rode the passenger coach and was thrilled at the speed of the train. It was as exhilarating as riding a racing horse and an unbelievable contrast to foot travel. Sally would often join him at Wahkiacus, as they both relished the luxury of this travel.

There was a word that describes Skookum, and that was "foxy." It surprised him that the white man often could see through his ways. He would try to arrange his visits to the mill so that he would arrive just before lunch which was really dinner in a logger's life. He would stand around until some lumberjack would invite him into the cookhouse to eat with them, he never needed to be asked twice. While the cost was small, the management finally ruled that the man who invited him in to eat would be charged with the meal, which meant he had no more invitations. But then he began coming to the mill with fruit to sell to the men. If the buyer felt he had gotten a good bargain, he sometimes broke down and invited Skookum in to eat.

One day Skookum tied his horses down near the planing mill and walked up to see the men. One was his saddle horse and other his pack horse, well loaded with baskets of grapes. During his visit the horses, while tramping around, got into a yellow jacket's nest and began bucking and rearing; and although Skookum ran to untie the horses, cursing in English, Indian, and jargon, they broke loose and tore down the railroad tracks scattering grapes all the way.

Homer Mitchell used to know Skookum well. He walked through Skookum's place on his way to his grandfather's homestead down the river, and Skookum was always eager to visit. He showed Homer his beautiful beaded buckskin suit and the fine feather head dress. He had been to Washington, D. C., twice, and he never tired of telling of meeting President Theodore Roosevelt on one of his visits and President Taft on another. He went back on behalf of Indian interests in the huckleberry fields, and on Mount Adams the fields marked, "For Indians Only," are the result of those visits.

O. P. Kreps of Glenwood told of Skookum, whom his family knew well, as they began renting spring pasture land from Skookum in 1916 and continued to do so until he died in 1923.

The Kreps' people knew all the Klickitat Indians, and on the annual trips of the Indians to the huckleberry fields on Mount Adams, many of the Klickitats, Spearfish, Celilo, and Rock Creek Indians camped at the Kreps place, and it was common to find fifty to one hundred Indians in camp. The family often gave food to the Indians which they paid for in huckleberries on their return trip. The Indians were honest; they did not forget a confidence or ever forget a friend.

The youngsters in the Kreps family always looked forward to the annual trip of the Indians, riding single file on their ponies with pack ponies, down the two-mile lane in the valley below the ranch. Squaws were wrapped in blankets, with papooses still in their "te-ca" boards hung on their backs. When camp was made, these papooses in their "te-ca" boards were removed from the squaws' backs, and boards and all were leaned against a handy tree. Skookum and his family were always part of this annual trip.

Kreps told of his family's experiences with cattle pastured on Skookum's place. "Skookum could not count but when we put cattle in pasture, he would ask; 'How many bells? How many blacks?' If any, 'How many whites?' and so on. We would show by holding up our fingers: seventeen fingers for seventeen bells and so on. The years we were there we never lost an animal that was not accounted for, and if a stray or two got into the pasture, Skookum knew it. He always helped to bring out the cattle, and on the day we started homeward, he would come as far as where we lunched so that he could eat with us before returning home. In driving the cattle, he always rode quite a ways behind, looking to the right and left to see that we did not lose any, many times spotting a calf that had gotten tired and lain down.

"We were always welcome at his house to visit or camp nearby. But he always said, 'White man no stay Indian's house.' I will say their house was always clean and neat. They did not use beds but had blankets in rolls along the walls, and they had no chairs so they sat on the bed rolls or on the floor."

One day Skookum Wallahee leaned on the top rail of his corral fence and looked at the dust that had been churned up yesterday by the hooves of the medicine men's horses when they were frightened by the piercing screams of Jennie, his 12-year-old daughter, when the vigorous treatment of the medicine men was more than she could bear in silence.

Just yesterday morning, but it seemed so long ago, when young Ollie Kreps had come to check the cattle in the leased pasture, Skookum had gone out to tell him that Jennie was sick and the shamans had come to make her well. That explained the bell ringing, chanting, and paroxysms of coughing that ended in earsplitting screams. He knew that Ollie was surprised to see him so agitated and broken out in a heavy sweat, as Indian men prided themselves on not showing their emotions. Only the women did that. But he just could not bear it when Jennie called to him for help and he could do nothing for her.

The medicine men had promised him that they could make Jennie well. They tried to work the poison from her body by massaging up her legs, body, and arms. They had cinched a manila cord about her waist so tight that it bruised her flesh and rivulets of blood oozed out. It had to be tight to keep the poison from slipping back. They would work up her body and when it reached the top of her head, it would be "poof, all gone." Only it was not gone, and he just could not watch when it made her cough until she had no breath left.

That night Jennie died. The white folks called it TB. According to Indian custom he had the right to take the lives of the medicine men because they had failed to make Jennie well again. But what good would that do? It would not bring Jennie back.

He turned and looked down across the meadow. There at the bend of the river, under those big pine trees, he could see a little mound of fresh dirt. That was where they had buried Jennie just as it was getting dark last night. He was glad that the darkness had prevented anyone from seeing the tears slipping down his cheeks.

The women had dressed Jennie in her favorite dress, the one with the pink rosebuds sprinkled over the blue cloth. Then they had combed and braided her long black hair, after which they had wrapped her in that new blue blanket that he had given two ponies for. His white neighbors had come and made a coffin out of bright new boards from the mill.

His family, like most of the Indians of the Northwest, believed that the wild rose bush possesses some kind of charm to keep away evil spirits, so when someone is in sickness or death, wild rose bushes are cut and walls, floors, windows, and doors are all carefully brushed. His sister's boys had dug the grave, and carried the little coffin down to where they all met and with the ritual prayers and wailing of the Indian custom and the Christian prayers of their closest white neighbor, they had buried his last child.

He had lost other children, but he did not tell of his early days to his white neighbors, but Jennie was different and maybe he was too. She had been a companion to him, even though she was a girl. She had walked with him, ridden with him, and even cooked for him when his two squaws were gone, as they were this morning. His heart was heavy when he thought about how thin Jennie had become. She had grown too tired to walk with him, or even ride with him to the company store. The last few days he had seen her cough until blood ran down in trickles from the corners of her mouth.

He wondered why this had happened to Jennie. He had used double magic when he gave her the name of Jennie so she would be like Jennie Wright, pretty, healthy, and always ready with a happy smile and friendly greeting, or like Jennie Stearns, his nearest neighbor, always so kind and willing to be of help. But the magic had not worked.

Maybe he should have talked to Mrs. Wright about what to do for Jennie when she began to cough. She was the mother of the other Jennie and the wife of the first white man to bring his family into the valley, and they were the first white settlers that he had gotten to know. They had a big family of nine children, boys and girls, who always recovered from their sicknesses, even measles and colds. When George, his son, caught measles, Mrs. Wright told him not to put George in the sweat house or dunk him in the icy river. She had given him some simple remedies and even sent broth for George to eat. George recovered, but many of the children treated in the old traditional way did not. It was the way they had always treated their ills, but they had never had these new diseases until the white man came.

He walked over and sat down on the stump by his door. It made a good seat and he could lean against the house wall, watching the cattle grazing in the pasture down by the river. He could look down the river and see smoke rising from his Indian neighbor's early fire, or turn his head and see the steam from the Holmes' mill with its cluster of workmen's cottages. Here men would be at work cutting the big old pine trees into lumber for more white folks to come and build more homes.

It was a beautiful valley carved out in ages past from the rocky walls by the fast moving waters of the Klickitat River. The high 1700 foot east canyon wall was sheer and covered with a heavy growth of old pine and fir, while the west side, just as high, but not as sheer, with its rockier soil grew grasses and clumps of Garry Oaks. These hillsides were coveted by the cattlemen, because they offered early grazing for cattle and horses. Along the river, the valley floor opened up into meadows and fields with occasional groves of big old pine. These idyllic meadows invited a few Indians to agree to allotments, and a few white people took homesteads as soon as any land was available.

It was a beautiful valley with its unmolested wild flowers and birds, sheltered from the rough east wind. It had been the home of his ancestors as far back as he knew.

In the days when his pappy lived, Indians could go any-where, but now there were fences, and the old trails were plowed up, and you were not allowed in the fields. In the olden times he had been free to roam and hunt; now he was no longer free, and the game had become so scarce that there was little to hunt. All he had was this allotment, and he could ride only where the white man said he had permission. He looked about at his orchard and garden and felt a sense of pride when he remembered that the white folks envied him his apples, grapes, strawberries, and watermelons. But he was sad this morning and wondered what good it did him to be Skookum Wallahee, Chief of the Klickitats.

Klickitats! It was a word that once brought fear to other tribes in this Northwest country, and to the few white settlers who had moved into this newly explored land. It is an Indian word with the euphonious sound common to many such Indian words, but which when pronounced in sounds and syllables of the English language, took on a very different sound.

The meaning of the word has been lost in antiquity, but many feel the word represented the KLICK-I-TAT, KLICK-I-TAT sound made by their ponies' hooves, as they galloped away on their raiding ventures. Others say it is the sound made by the tumbling boulders in their fast moving streams, but many agree with Professor Edward Meaney in his history of Washington, when he says of the Puget Sound Indians, "occasionally they have been troubled by raids of warlike Indians from the Yakima country, whom they called Klickitats, meaning 'Robbers.'"

Among the local Indians in their own language, they are called "Whul-why-pums" who say their word means "beyond," and that is appropriate as they live beyond the mountains, beyond the plains, and beyond the river.

The tribe of Klickitat, of which Skookum Wallahee was un-disputed chief, lived in the area between Mt. Adams and Mt. St. Helens and the Columbia River in the valleys of the Lewis, White Salmon, and Klickitat Rivers with the Klickitat the most popular. With their small villages stretching along the Columbia to above Celilo Falls it became like a confederacy, and they were known as the Klickitat tribe. They were nomadic and were able to go far afield, after getting horses from tribes to the east. In the old days they and the Nez Perce were considered the two most powerful tribes in the Northwest. When the census was taken in 1850, their numbers were listed at 500. It is hard to say how accurate the figures are as they were a nomadic tribe and the census takers were not greatly concerned with statistics. Like other tribes, their numbers grew to be less as they suffered from the great epidemics of measles and small pox that decimated whole villages in the lower Columbia. Another deteriorating influence had been their inability to cope with the white man's alcohol.

Skookum was not the only one who wondered why things had gone the way they had. Usually the stories that were told made it seem that the whites were always right and the Indians were fit only for extinction. One Goldendale man told of his grandfather, who was known as an Indian hunter: "Upon Grandfather's return from an Indian skirmish, Grandmother asked if they had harmed the children, but he curtly answered 'Nits make lice' and that was the common attitude. She didn't dare to question him further."

The Klickitats were tall and straight-limbed, had small hands and feet, and were of rather fine features with the usual black hair and eyes. They generally wore their hair straight, cut with bangs to just above the eyes. This "hair-do" became known among the settlers until women as far away as Seattle refused to wear their hair in bangs as the Klickitats did. Many of the young Klickitat women were beautiful but had the tendency to become fat as they grew older, no doubt due to the heavy diet of salmon.

Skookum had a bad leg which gave him trouble. He told Mrs. Stearns that he had a bullet in his leg and told others that he had hurt it in a fall from a horse. One of his horses had sickened and died in his barn and to get it out, he hitched a team to the dead horse with a long rope. As he pulled the horse out, the team got frightened and swung about catching him in the bight of the rope and giving him a bad rope burn. His leg was never well again. He doctored it in Indian style, taking little coals of cedar bark and placing them around the sore place, burning holes in the flesh. When he was quite bad, his neighbors took him and his squaw to the doctor at The Dalles. The doctor recommended that they amputate the leg, and Skookum agreed, but his squaw said "No," so he came home and stayed until he died.

The day Skookum died was the fifteenth of December; it was cold and there was snow on the ground. An Indian came up to Klickitat and invited Art Vause, a long time friend of Skookum's to come to the wake, so Art and his nephew walked down the railroad track to Skookum's house and Art told of the experience.

"The door was closed and no one was about, so we knocked on the door and an usher came to greet us, but he detained us as he had to ask Skookum's spirit if we should be allowed to come in. He went to the corpse and put his hand to Skookum's mouth, rang a bell, and asked Jesus if the white men should come in. The spirit said 'yes' according to the usher, because we were very good 'tillicums.' There were about twenty Indians sitting around but no other whites. They had their moccasins off and a roaring fire in the stove. The medicine man insisted an evil spirit in the form of a coyote was trying to get Skookum's spirit so there was much bell ringing and commotion until the medicine man needed a recess. All this heat and smell was too much for my nephew, who got sick and had to be excused, while I remained for the rest of the ceremony. Skookum was dressed in full buckskin suit, and his formal headdress and was wrapped in a blanket. His head was resting on a little buckskin bag in which he had preserved his hair combings." The significance of these combings was never divulged and only conjecture can give it meaning. It was part of the body that they felt was needed in the spirit world.

That same night they buried him in a grave on his own property near the river. This was his request, because he wanted to be buried like a white man with a gravestone to mark the spot. However, the next year, according to Indian custom, his body was exhumed and his body wrapped in a new blanket and reburied. His tombstone carries the record of his age as seventy-five years and his death as December 15, 1923.

His older squaw continued to live on the place, but according to Skookum's wishes it was not leased. She lived on a few years, selling a few baskets. When she died, she was buried near Skookum's grave but with no marker. A nephew and niece inherited the land and later sold it to a white man.

Today the house is still occupied. The fruit trees, now old, send out their fragrant blooms each year and still produce some fruit. The land has become a development and was sold to eager buyers for homes along the river. In fact so eager are they that Skookum's gravestone is barely given room among the corn-stalks and squash vines in a garden, and the unmarked graves no longer indicate the resting places of other family members.

XXXII

An Indian Feast

The Indian Longhouse was the center of much of their ritual and worship.

The Indians have been taught by their forebearers to be appreciative of their gifts of salmon, roots, and berries, and feasts are given at the time of the first salmon and first roots each spring. These are held in the various long houses at Rock Creek or Satus. In the year 1951 Chief Tommie Kuni Thompson of the Wyams invited all neighboring Indians to come to their feast to honor the first salmon of the spring Chinooks. All Indians were invited and non-Indian visitors were invited to watch.

The Indians came from the east and the west. They were moving in from the Klickitat and the White Salmon, from the north and the south. The salmon were beginning to run and these folk were coming in to the Wyams for a salmon feast, where Chief Tommie Kuni Thompson was the revered leader, and where he would act as host. The feast was held in the long house at Celilo and as the strangers came, they brought their blankets and their big shawl-wrapped bundles, and these they lay along the walls around the long house. Each blanket roll makes a little camp site where "comers," as the strangers were called, could change clothes for the three days of the feast.

Word had come that the salmon were coming up the river like "ho-lee," the west wind. The salmon feast, called Ka-wit in the Indian language, is basically a religious festival to give thanks for sending the salmon. They wait for the first fish to be caught at the Falls, which is then cut in the traditional prescribed manner and served ceremoniously.

To get a better understanding of the Indians' feeling about this ceremony, it is best to refer to Martha Ferguson McKeown, who was the only white member of the Wyams and has written of it in *Come to My Salmon Feast*.

"The Wyams have been watching the mud swallows. Henry Thompson, the sub-chief, has been watching for the birds, which were the harbingers of salmon and when watching told their story. He said, 'The mud swallows are the spirits of five beautiful maidens, who once built a dam under a great rock bridge across the Columbia River. They built this dam so that all the salmon would have to stay down below the bridge. They wanted to help their friends, the Chinooks, who lived near the mouth of the Wauna, the great river. They did not seem to care that the Wyams were starving for salmon above the bridge.'

"When Mr. Coyote, whose Indian name was Speelyai, discovered this dam across the Columbia, he started to dig. He dug so fast and so hard that the bridge fell in, making the cascades in the Columbia. Then Mr. Coyote, who does both good and bad just like all human beings turned those beautiful maidens into mud swallows. Now, the mud swallows have to fly above the first salmon that come up the river each spring. That is their way of asking forgiveness of the Wyams for the harm they once tried to do them.'"

In front of the long house the women have put a long cutting table, where the men put the fish as they bring them up from the Falls. Here the women scale and clean the salmon, split them down the backbone, and run sharp willow cooking sticks up through the flesh. The sticks and the wood for the fires have already been blessed by the chief. Spring salmon must always be cooked under an open sky. It must be touched by the wind, the good air, and the warm sunshine. "Noo-sok" is their name for salmon when it is red in the springtime and "me-too-la" is the name for old salmon after the flesh has turned white in the fall.

The women could hear the songs and prayers in the long house while they cooked the salmon, always according to the old rules. Pieces of arrowwood were used to hold the salmon from curling. These sticks were peeled and flattened on two sides to keep them from turning. Then sharpened on both ends, they were stuck in the ground. The flesh side of the salmon must always be turned first toward the fire, then the skin side.

Chief Tommie Thompson saw to it that his guests were properly cared for. The great salmon feast started when he rang his little brass bell.

His helpers carrying the great rolls of tule mats came in and half circled the floor. They stopped in front of the chief while he blessed the mats, and then laid these "Indian tablecloths" down the center. The helpers carried in empty plates and cups as they set the places, always moving from right to left as the earth turns.

The first cooking was then taken from the fire and Chief Thompson opened the feast with these words:

"Our Father we greet Thee. These children of earth come here to share thanks today. We come to pay tribute to all hungry people in the name of the Great Almighty."

Then all the Indians raised their hands and said "Ee-ah." In their language this means "Amen."

River water had been brought and filled each cup. When each person had taken a sip, the chief rang the bell to summon the salmon for the feast.

The chief's wife entered carrying the first beautiful salmon on its cooking stick. She was followed by other women of the great river. They too have been chosen for the blessing and sharing. This was a great honor that has come to them, because they follow the ways of the River Indians. Over and over again the chief would say, "The old ways are the best ways for my people."

Behind the chief's wife and other women were the strange "comers." Often they did not know about the old ways and the meaning of the salmon feast at Celilo Falls. They did not always understand that these Indians must "pay tribute to all hungry people in the name of the Almighty." No Wyam might eat until every hungry stranger had been fed. Chief Thompson said this is the law, "Given to the old, old people of long ago by our God, the Great Almighty."

During the great salmon feast of 1951 three sittings of "comers" lined both sides of the tule mats. Some even started "stick" games out on the grounds, but the "true believers" quietly took their places on the raised seats at the east end of the long house. There they listened and prayed while the old chief blessed the water and the salmon for each setting of "comers."

No Wyam ate until all of the visitors had been served. During the serving not one of the chief's helpers failed to circle from right to left as the earth turns.

The old River Indians loved God, the Almighty, but they were afraid of Him. He was an Indian God. They believed that He would be quick to punish them if they broke His laws, but Chief Thompson believed that He was always listening to him. That is why the old chief would never talk about salmon in any language except his own. "At the time of Creation," the old chief said, "this great food was given to us and since then the Wyams have always tried to stay on the right side, according to the Almighty."

When the people had eaten their fill, the chief again rang his bell and the old Indians stood, turned to the left, bowed to the bell and the drum, then turned back to the east and began to sing, "How Thankful Are We To The Almighty." After each verse they stretched their hands higher toward the sky. By the end of the song they were all standing with their arms toward the sky, as they thanked the Almighty for sending them the great food of salmon.

Among the women that day stood a woman praying, who was Vameen-wat. Her great uncle was Spencer, the brave Indian scout who helped the Americans during the Indian wars of the 1850's. Spencer's wife and six children had been killed by the whites as they were fleeing to safety when mistaken for hostiles. He continued as a faithful scout, but took the name of "Sa-wee," which means the Lonely One.

After the men had gone to their games and visiting, the children to their running and playing, the chief to his resting and prayers until it was time to dress up in his chief's regalia, the women could eat the first food they had had since the previous day. They had been trained to serve others first.

The big drum called "kool-kool-us" was made from the hide of the swiftest horse that ever raced on the Warm Springs Reservation; its voice so deep it could be heard for miles.

Chief Thompson said, "When this great drum is sounded, the songs of thanksgiving from our bodies and souls sound down through the heart of Mother earth. Then the great heart of the Almighty opens with understanding. He leans down and listens. He hears the songs and prayers of His earth people."

The rest of the day and night were spent in the various dances and visiting, always with special prayers to let the Almighty know that they were appreciative of His gifts. They have known of these special gifts down through the years, for the old people have told them and their parents and grandparents the myths of the distant past.

XXXIII

Arts and Crafts

The beautiful basket made by one of Skookum's squaws.

The Indians were always skillful with their hands, as attested to by the great number of arrowheads that have been found near the mouth of the Little Klickitat. With their primitive tools, much skill and patience must have been needed.

One essential skill that had to be learned was the preparation of the hides of the game killed for use as for bedding or clothing. First the hide was soaked in a solution of ashes and water until the hair loosened and could be scraped off. Then the brains of the animal were worked into the hide to soften it. How they learned to use the brains and passed the knowledge around will never be known.

The hide is then laced to a frame where it can be worked and scraped some more, and the slack taken up by the laces. When finished, the hide is soft and pliable as well as white in color.

For some purposes such as ceremonial dress, it is whitened even more by the use of marl earth or white clay being rubbed in. To make it more durable, it is placed in the smoke of smoldering rotten wood, which gives it the Indian tan color. Unless so treated, a moccasin or shirt would become stiffer after wetting. It is also what gives it that pungent odor associated with Indians.

The women had to make the garments. The Klickitat Indians wore deer, elk, or mountain goat skins made into rude shirts with loose sleeves; leggings reached halfway up the thigh, fastened by strings to a belt around the waist, and moccasins of buckskin. Over this was worn a robe of elk or buffalo skin. The woman's garment reached almost to the ankles, and over this was a cape of skin. These were their ceremonial clothes and were decorated with fringe, porcupine quills, or shells. After the coming of the white man, they made designs with beads, shells, elk teeth, or whatever they felt was attractive.

For common wear the men might wear a "G" string and a hat of fur, while a woman wore a skirt of shredded cedar bark and a hat made like a small embricated basket. After the Hudson's Bay Company came, they were able to obtain cloth, from which they made "Mother Hubbard" type dresses out of the calicoes and colored Hudson Bay blankets.

The Indian women had another duty also, and that was basket making. For the ones made up in the huckleberry fields, they used Western Red Cedar bark, but this kind has not been made in recent years, as cedar trees have become scarcer. The baskets were easily made and took only an hour or two, once the bark had been brought into camp, and ranged in size from one- to ten-gallon capacity. They made excellent containers for transporting berries to their homes or to the ranchers to repay earlier promises.

In order to begin making a basket, a woman peeled from a live tree a strip of bark double the length and slightly wider than the diameter of the basket desired. Then she marked a sharp pointed oval across the middle of the length of the strip. Along this line she made two parallel cuts about half an inch apart halfway through the inner bark and removed this layer. This made a hinge so that when the two ends of the strip were brought together the basket was almost finished. The oval became the bottom and all she needed to complete the job was to take some lacings made from the inner bark of cedar, fasten the sides together, and lace in a ring of cedar root around the top.

Another type, the Klickitat basket, as it is commonly called, is rigid and very durable. Some are still in use after a hundred years. One woman, when asked how old her beautiful basket was, replied, "It was her mama's mama and her mama's mama," repeating these words for several more generations of mamas. The Indians still use this type of basket, and the young folks, of whom Nettie Kuneki the granddaughter of Sally Wahkiacus is one, are learning this basketry. When the settlers first came, they saw many of these baskets and did not give them the appreciation they deserved. It was the same with a young boy who had grown up in the village of Klickitat with Indian boys as friends, when as a serviceman in the U. S. Army he visited the Natural History Museum in New York and saw the long shelf of Klickitat baskets prominently displayed, realized they were objects to cherish.

This basket took an infinite amount of painstaking time and skill. It was made from dried squaw grass (bear grass) which grows abundantly in the high country and was the grass the squaws gathered when huckleberrying in the mountains. The framework, coil type, was made of some sort of pliable root such as willow or cedar. The start was made in the center of the bottom, the basket progressing outward and upward in ever widening circles until the desired size and shape was attained, the grass and split roots so tightly woven together that the basket, when completed was watertight. In bygone days the Indian women actually cooked in them by the hot stone method before they got kettles from trading with white men. Designs were woven into the baskets with grasses colored by natural dyes such as bright yellow from the root of yellow Oregon grape as well as other colors from pounded-up roots and flowers, black from soot, and browns from the mud of mineral springs. Dyes were made from minerals; a clear green was obtained from the slime found on rocks in stream beds, yellow was made from a tea of roots of the Oregon grape, and red was made from alder. Ethnologists are certain the Klickitats learned some of their basketry from south of the Columbia and assert that that is where they had lived in fairly recent times, yet Martin Spedis claimed his forebearers had lived continuously at Wishram. Could it have been a small nomadic band that lived elsewhere and brought home knowledge of basket making to share with the others?

The Klickitats made a bag called the Cornhusk Bag which was made of twined weave overlaid with false embroidery. The threads which were to form the warp were suspended from some convenient object, then the weaver began to fill in the weft, thus working from the bottom of the bag to the top or edge. The weft threads were woven in pairs: as one thread crossed over a strand of warp, the other went under it; then before the next strand of warp was reached, the two strands of weft thread crossed one over the other. The greater part of the bag, usually all but a span of about two inches at the bottom and less at the top, was covered with false embroidery woven in with the weft. A thread of the false embroidery material was twisted over the weft as it crossed the warp strand in such a way that the false embroidery showed on the inside of the bag only, where a new thread was inserted or an old thread broken off. On the outside the warp and weft were entirely covered. A bag of plain twined weave showed a smooth surface made of regular spaced threads lying at a very slight angle from the horizontal. When twining had been overlaid by the false embroidery, the same even surface was maintained, but the threads lay in opposite directions and at a slightly greater angle. The top of the bag was finished by the simple method of turning down the warp strands and binding them well with the weft.

The technique of plain weaving is one of the oldest types known and is found almost all over the world.

In older bags the basic warp was made of Indian hemp, and the false embroidery of bear grass. In later bags the false embroidery was made of husks of corn with geometric patterns used.

They loved to decorate their garments with designs done with beadwork. Beads became available through the Hudson's Bay Company, which carried stocks of Chinese, French, and Viennese beads, as well as the ordinary small white or colored beads. Later even the store at Blockhouse carried sample cards of numbered beads which could be ordered from The Dalles and Portland. Necklaces and ornaments of all kinds were cleverly designed and well made. Many articles are still in existence, but the cotton thread which is their basis is fragile and easily broken.

At housekeeping Indian women differed just as do white women, and they had to be more ingenuous and resourceful. Because they had no refrigeration, the foods had to be dried and smoked and kept in bags hanging in their teepees and must have been treated regularly with smoke from their cooking fires. Their salmon, after being prepared as pemmican, could be stored in sacks and covered in a sheltered spot. Their dishes were never washed except that the dogs were allowed to lick them clean. Their clothing was not washed, but sometimes the ceremonial clothes were cleaned with marl rubbed in, and they seldom bathed except for certain purification rites or using the therapeutic treatment of the sweat house. Their bedding was furs or grass mats rolled up and pushed against the walls in daytime when they were used as comfortable seats.

Stone tools and implements are found throughout the United States since little, if any, metal was used before the coming of the white man. But other materials were used by the pre-white contact Indians such as wood, clay, shell, bone, bark, reeds and grasses, copper, mica, animal teeth, feathers, wool, and hair of various animals.

The stone sculpture of the Pacific Northwest comprises a number of distinguishable styles. It also appears in a variety of different forms and objects, and it is often of a size larger and more impressive sculpturally than that of any other American Indian art north of Mexico.

Unlike stone carvings from other American Indian areas and evidently typical of the Columbia River Valley are a considerable number of sculptures which served no utilitarian purpose. Of these are a variety of carved figures, representing human, animal, geometric, and abstract forms.

It is not possible at present time to date these sculptures. A reasonable antiquity can be claimed for several of them. They were all made before the coming of the white explorers, traders, and settlers. The Indians who have inhabited this region have no knowledge of their origin or meaning.

Some of the sculptures, especially those of the Columbia River Valley, were associated with burials or cremation pits. These were found near or on the surface, sometimes in caves or graveyard sites.

Several features of Northwest stone sculpture must be considered before its aesthetic qualities are understood or appreciated. The useful objects were not more efficient because of the sculpture on them. But those may have added a spiritual quality.

Wakemap

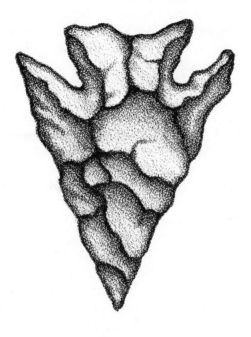

*An Indian arrowhead, one of hundreds discovered at
Wakemap (Wŏk-e-mop) Mound.*

The stratified mound which Lewis and Clark saw along the
Columbia, which they said appeared artificial was, no doubt,
the midden that came to be called Wakemap. This mound covered an area 350 feet long by 270 feet wide and 20 feet high. It
probably started as a camp site. As refuse accumulated and
became unbearable to the inhabitants, dirt would be carried and
spread over the offending deposit. Their possessions would be
meager but as the Indians number increased their artifacts became more plentiful—bone and antler implements, especially
dice, and ornaments appeared. Near the top of the midden

varieties increased but bone and antler were not found. Knives and "dagger points" are recent as are artifacts of clay. Trade goods were found only on the surface. "Dagger points" were narrow blades with a stem shaped from almost circular to diamond. The mound had been deserted before the arrival of Lewis and Clark, even though the area was not abandoned.

The age of the mound is a controversial subject. Carbon 14 method shows an age of 1,000 years and geological evidence 2,000 years, while the art-producing culture is estimated at 200 to 1,500 years.

Even though Vine Deloria, Jr., member of the Sioux, author and worker for Indian causes, felt that the anthropologists have done the Indians more harm than good, it is through their work that we will learn more about the cultural lives of these early aborigines who lived in this area now submerged by The Dalles Dam.

By agreement with the University of Washington, holder of a contract with the National Park Service for excavations in The Dalles area, the Oregon Archaeological Society was granted permission to excavate under supervision. Members were not permitted to sell any specimens or dispose of them without permission. Scientists, Dr. Warren Caldwell, Dr. Douglas, and Dr. L. A. Cressman were in charge of the work.

Dr. Cressman alone found 102 specimens of pestles and mauls. Mauls are not to be confused with pestles as they have a flaring base and are used in driving wedges in splitting wood into planks, while pestles are used in the preparation of food. Many more pestles than mortars were found because some wooden bowls were used and naturally decayed.

Wakemap was not a burial site and the articles found there were a true cross-section of implements used in normal everyday life. One artifact in great abundance was the small triangular corner-notched arrow point, found in all The Dalles sites.

Objects of art found along the Columbia attest to a high degree of culture. The quality of the stone used has a bearing on the quality of the product, for the harder the stone is to work, the more intense must be the desire. The Columbia stone is one of the most difficult and the precision with which the objects were made shows considerable aptitude.

The pieces show certain characteristics: the stylized ribs and frequently the whole vertebrae, the crescent mouth and grinning face, elaborate hair ornamentation, bulging and circled eyes, as well as the massiveness of form, attest to their origin. The Spedis owl is common and found only between the John Day River and the Cascades.

The word "Wakemap" is an anglicized word from "Wuq'emap" which means ogress or old woman, and rhymes with "Wok-em-up."

A number of middens and burial sites have been excavated. Many artifacts from far away were found, such as pipestone from Minnesota, turquoise from the Southwest, copper from Michigan or Alaska, graphite from Montana, and dentalium from Vancouver Island, all showing the extensiveness of the trade that went on here at old Wishram.

Today's Indian

Cody, the grandson of Sally Wahkiacus.

As the 20th Century is drawing to a close, the Indian problem is still with us. It is true that their numbers are increasing and their general living and health conditions have improved. Their life styles have changed as has the attitude of the whites toward the Indians. They have become American citizens with all the rights and duties pertaining thereto. They still do not want to farm, but they must attend school to learn English and to read and write.

The relations between the U. S. Government and the Yakima Tribe is a set of rules and traditions too complex to be changed with the stroke of a pen. The Indians, themselves, are not agreed as to what the relation should be, and there are always those, both red and white, that are trying to stir up discontent. The young boys and men keep telling that they want the old ways back, as any young buck will tell you after listening to the soapbox orators. But he really does not want to give up motor boats, cars, and electric lights, ready-made clothes or the food of the supermarkets. He doesn't want to give up the Health Clinics that have saved the lives of many of their young children. He doesn't want to live in smoke-filled teepees in winter's cold. What he does want is an impossible idyllic life that would give him the best of the new with the freedoms of the old.

The Indian families, whose stories were told, lived fairly comfortable lives as far as food was concerned. They liked their neighbors, and their neighbors had kind regard for them. The young children went to the same school as the white children and most of them did well; they participated in school athletics, and often were star performers, but there was no incentive to induce continuation in trade schools or college as they had no examples to follow.

The stories were told to show their feelings are much the same as those of the white man. He has his loves and his hates, his jealousies and his pride, his vices and his loyalties. They need to be understood and appreciated.

In working toward a new solution to this whole Indian problem it is well to recall once again the unsuccessful efforts that were made in the past so as not to go on making the same mistakes again.

When the first colonists came to America, they found the Indians friendly, with very few that were hostile. The Puritans would not have been able to survive their first winter without the help of the Friendlies who showed them where and how to fish, what plants and roots were edible, and where to hunt for game. They even shared their meagre supplies of corn. The Puritans needed to learn what the wilderness could offer, and they needed kindness, and the Indians gave them both.

The tremendous growth of the United States, the expansion westward, the development of manufacturing and machinery resulted in a period of feverish prosperity. After the usual excesses the collapse came in 1837. The people out of work or those unable to pay their debts crowded the road to the west to seek new opportunities.

In the 1830's the government passed the Removal Act, which it felt would be the answer to the problem. It moved all Indians living east of the Mississippi River to the Great Plains on the west side of the big river, the Mississippi. This land was to be segregated for them alone and to be known as the Indian Territory, with protection promised from encroachment. This trek proved to be full of suffering and hardship until it was known as the Trail of Tears.

The land proved to be better than anticipated and the promises to keep it for the Indians could not be kept. It became a part of the State of Oklahoma and opened for homesteading.

Because of the great influx of settlers to the west, it was realized something had to be done for the Pacific Northwest, and so Isaac Stevens was sent out to Washington as its Governor, and as an Indian Agent, and Railroad Surveyor to get Indians to be willing to give up land and to settle on reservations.

The Indians west of the Cascades proved to be fairly tractable if they could live on reservations in their own area, while those east of the mountains were averse to giving up any of their land, but were threatened until they gave up at the Council Meeting held at Walla Walla, and the Yakima Reservation was set up for the fourteen Confederated Tribes. It was one of three set up with a fourth added later.

All tribal societies were forbidden and the Indians were to become Wards of the State, with annuities and help for twenty years, at which time they were expected to be self-sufficient.

The boundaries were set up by white men who had never been over the land. The land had never been surveyed, and Indian names were used in places not clearly defined or accurate. Misunderstandings and greedy decisions resulted on both sides.

To better manage, agents had been appointed by the President for the various reservations. Many proved to be more interested in acquiring their own fortunes than in doing the work to which they had been assigned. To improve this situation, it was decided to let different church bodies be responsible for recommending agents overseeing their specified tribes. That is how Father Wilbur, as he was called as a Methodist Missionary, became responsible for the Yakimas.

People being what they are, wrangling and jealousies among the church bodies proved this was not the answer. One story shows how little understanding there was among "the folks back home" when in a missionary barrel there arrived forty pairs of garters for a tribe that did not wear a single pair of stockings.

Father Wilbur, while agent at Fort Simcoe, showed that he knew how to handle Indians and did much to teach them in school. He never carried a weapon and was a strict disciplinarian. He helped them develop a fine herd of cattle marked with the ID brand, which was stupidly sold off by the military when they were given charge of Fort Simcoe.

The first immigrants began to move into the valley in the late 1850's. It was a beautiful valley then, covered everywhere with rich, luxuriant bunch grass—a regular cattleman's paradise. From the Columbia hills to the timber covered Simcoes stretched an immense pasture, but in a few years a thousand fences separated that fine pasture into grain fields.

The government had built a wagon road in 1856 from Fort Simcoe across the Simcoe Range to Fort Dalles. The same year, they built a fort at Spring Creek seven miles northwest of what is now Goldendale. It was garrisoned by a troop of U. S. Calvary until 1860 and kept in readiness until 1870.

After pressure, Congress adopted the Allotment Act in 1887. It was felt that if each Indian had a piece of land as his own, he would be more content and interested in raising a garden or grain to supplement his dwindling resources for roots and berries. But the white man did not understand that the Indian does not possess the same feeling toward land or work that a white man does.

The Indian has always been averse to farming, nor does he have Puritanical beliefs in work but instead wants freedom of action without the regimentation required in agricultural work.

He thinks differently than a white man, whether due to his genes or his environment is for the experts to decide.

It was reluctantly agreed that the Allotment System was not working out as had been hoped. In 1914, when the rolls were closed, 4,506 allotments had been given out, which meant 444,000 acres had been granted. Difficulties arose over inheritances because only those with at least one-fourth Indian blood from an ancestor of the fourteen tribes was to hold land. When on the reservation, they must be called Yakimas, when elsewhere they could be recognized as of their original tribe.

The Indians were not agreed as to what they wanted, but most thought they should have power to run their own affairs and make their own mistakes. In 1934, powers were given to organize along tribal lines. Since that time they have had a General Council, elected by a majority vote of the tribal members, who have the right to participate and initiate measures, while any male member over eighteen may vote, and a majority determines an issue.

The General Council's origin is ancient. Originally, the people were called together by the chiefs to decide what should be done. Such rights had been taken away from them when they became wards of the state.

The Yakima Tribal Council is now the business committee of the tribe and is composed of fourteen members, representing the fourteen original tribes. Members of this body are elected by the General Council. Power to transact all tribal business, excepting that expressly reserved, was delegated to them in 1944.

The Yakimas have their own Code of Laws regulating conduct between its own members on the reservation, but the ten major crimes are handled by the Department of Justice, through the Federal courts, although this may soon be reversed.

Allotment roles made in the 1880's and 1890's were the only record of membership for many years, and the need arose for an up-to-date list. In 1945, the General Council asked Congress to help include members living on public-domain allotments within the ceded area as well as those on the reservation.

Occasionally a member gets payment from the tribal funds coming from grazing rights or sale of timber. If anyone owns an old allotment, he receives whatever the allotment brings.

In 1954, the Indian Nation authorized expenditures of its own funds to give high school graduates scholarship assistance. They may go to schools of their choice. This was a long step as not so long ago many of the "old braids" were opposed to the young people going to white schools or to learning English.

There had been much confusion about citizenship, as Indians had been granted it if they earned Patents on their allotments. In 1924, to correct this, all Indians born in the U. S. were given citizenship. Although they do not pay taxes on their reservation lands, on other property they pay as any other citizen does.

Some improvement was made on reservation land with the participation in irrigation projects which increased production of fruits and vegetables and made the land more valuable. The initial high costs were met by sale of lands.

In the early days of the reservation, the whites were glad that much of the land retained was timbered, as clearing land with primitive tools was both slow and hazardous. The Indians had been offered $400,000 for their timber and had wisely refused to sell, but no one had any idea of the astronomical figures that timber would rise to in the 1970's.

The Indian Service had been reluctant to sell timber, wanting to conserve it as a resource. The Washington State Forestry Department had made a study of harvesting Ponderosa Pine under sustained-yield practices. When the result of the study came to the Indian's attention, they realized their forests could be kept both vigorous and productive and decided to make sales under such a program. They mark the trees carefully, police the logging, and study the results.

There was some feeling in the tribe to do their own lumber manufacturing the way the Warm Springs tribe was doing, while others felt it would bring additional problems as it did to the tribes in Arizona. One old Indian explained it thus: "The forest belongs to all the Indians that are enrolled. Every buck would feel that he had a right to a job just as other bucks did, whether he was qualified or not. This would mean too many bucks working, cost too much money."

Because fishing was still important to their lives, there had been much objection over the proposed Bonneville Dam for fear it would interrupt the runs of salmon. Fish ladders were promised to eliminate the danger of destroying fish life. When engineers began working on plans for The Dalles Dam at Celilo, the feeling ran so high that new sites were explored in hopes that the Celilo site with the old fishing grounds promised at the Walla Walla Treaty could be spared. However, alternate sites presented insurmountable difficulties. The Celilo site was used and recompense was paid to the Indians.

Early in the discussions, the government removed the Indian dead from the burial islands that would be flooded in the impounded waters of the new dam. Identified dead were removed to new graves, and the unmarked bones were buried in a single concrete vault in a new cemetery not far from the dam.

Then came the question of recompense. Because the future runs of salmon could not be foretold accurately figuring out the worth of the salmon that would be lost to the Indian fisheries could be done only by a rough estimate.

The result for the Yakimas was as follows: the Yakima tribe listed 4,300 men, women and children. Each was to be allowed $3,270 as his share. Saluskin, as Tribal Council Chairman, advised the tribal members to retain the money in the tribal fund, but the members outvoted him, and it was distributed to the individuals. The Warm Springs Indians retained their payments in the tribal moneys and have used them to build up businesses until they now rate as one of the wealthiest tribes in the nation.

It was their own decision. It is hard to say whether the payment per share to the individual brought the greater good or the annual payments made to the 2,300 members of the Confederated Tribes of the Warm Springs. All depends on what the individuals did with their initial payments.

Economic and health problems remain acute for both tribal and urban Indians. Along with unemployment, health remains a chronic problem for today's Indians. Many still live in inadequate houses with sub-standard sanitation, and as a people, they are prone to certain diseases and suffer more severely from them. While the general health level of Indians has improved, it is still below the average level of the United States population, according to government reports. Infant mortality has improved with the help of Health Clinics with their care and information, but old traditions still persist.

At The Dalles Hospital, just a few years ago, a young Indian couple brought in a very sick tiny baby, suffering from a severe cold. Upon accepting the baby, the nurse was about to remove the baby's cap, but found it to be dried chicken manure. Upon inquiry, the mother admitted that it was intended to cure the baby of lice. It sounds revolting to antiseptic-trained people, but if one is realistic, one wonders what she could have done under the circumstances. They still need help in health and sanitation.

Many of the younger generation wanted to leave the reservation and find work and homes in the city. The Bureau of Indian Affairs set up a relocation bureau, which offers help in transportation and adjustment in a new place. Many have made the transition successfully, while others have found themselves stranded in an alien world. The BIA estimates that a third of them return home.

About one half of the Indian population live outside the 268 reservations, yet they have not disappeared into the general population, since they still maintain their own identity. The younger folk have become more militant and differ from the older and more traditional Indian leaders, some of whom have felt that the younger people would endanger needed federal support. One of the deadliest confrontations and one that widened the gap between the young and the old began in 1973, at the village of Wounded Knee in South Dakota's Pine Ridge Reservation. This same village was chosen as the psychological choice for the remembrance of the massacre in 1890 of 50 to 300 Indians by the U. S. Calvary.

On February 27, a force of about 200 armed Indians, led by Indian Movement Organizers, took over Wounded Knee. It began as an Indian confrontation in an Indian-against-Indian dispute where the younger militants accused the older leaders of corruption. For seventy-one days the militants held out to advance their demands for self-determination, for hearings on U. S. Treaties, and for a Congressional Investigation of the government's treatment of the Indians. By the time it was over two militants were dead, one U. S. Marshall was seriously wounded, and the issues, themselves, were lost in a maze of hatred and bitterness.

If any good comes out of such confrontations, it is hard to say, but according to Wilcomb Washburn, the author, it was an important symbol of "a new and raucous Indian voice, a voice which celebrated separatism instead of integration, political activism instead of dignified acquiescence, repudiation of white goals and values, and the rejection of existing tribal organization."

Everyone who knows Indians is deeply aware of one problem that seems common to all the tribes and that is their reaction to alcohol. With them, there seems to be no moderation and they end up in a drunken stupor. White people have tried to help through laws, compassion, and religion, but to little avail.

To illustrate, the situation is often told of Ira Hayes, a Pima Indian. He was one of the Marines that had raised the flag on Iwo Jima and had become a symbol of bravery. Upon their return to the U. S. these boys had been feasted, feted and bemedalled. Then Ira was forgotten in the general stream of new heroes. He wandered home to the arid deserts of Arizona and became destitute without work and without hope. He had been a good soldier. It was not only his courage that had been honored, for he had been a good boy, a good Indian, and a good soldier. He had abandoned his "Indianness" during these years of military service and now, coming back, he was unprepared for life on the reservation. He had nothing to sustain him. He became the drunken Ira Hayes. He drowned in a drainage ditch, in two inches of water in the desert. He had needed someone to befriend him in his discouragement. That is what an Indian needs as well as the white man.

Indians are beginning to realize that it is they who can be of the greatest help in this addiction that destroys the potential abilities and the lives of many of their young people. One step in the right direction by the Yakimas is the setting up of an Indian Alcoholics Annonymous. It must be Indian-for-Indian, if it is to be successful.

Now that they have the authority, we find them giving time and effort to renewing tribal feasts and rituals. Care and appreciation are being given to unique crafts that will be preserved. Antique costumes are being saved and the old arts and crafts are being taught to the younger folk, to help them to feel pride in their old culture. More cultural centers will be developed where all Americans can see and learn of the fine baskets, beadwork and all the other items that can be appreciated by all.

Fishing rights will continue to be problems for both red and white men. Until greed can be held in check the grievances will continue.

For those of us who have admired our Indian friends and grieved over the problems that have befallen them, we continue to hope for understanding and friendliness. We believe that we have a wonderful land and that time will temper extreme demands. We can and must work together to continue to give us the country that we love.

BIBLIOGRAPHY

American Heritage . . . . Book of Indians
Atwell, Jim . . . . Columbia River History, Volume I
Atwell, Jim . . . . Columbia River History, Volume II
Baker, Burt Brown . . . . The McLoughlin Empire
Balch, F. H. . . . . The Bridge of the Gods
Ballou, Robert . . . . Early Klickitat Valley Days
Berkhofer, Robert . . . . Salvation and the Savage
Backholm, Stephen . . . . The Indians of Western Oregon
Boyd, James P. . . . . Indian Wars
Brogan, Phil . . . . East of the Cascades
Bunnell, Clarence O. . . . . Legends of the Klickitats
Clark, Ella E. . . . . Indian Legends of the Pacific
                                       Northwest
Clarke, S. A. . . . . Pioneer Days of Oregon History,
                                       Volume II
Carter, E. Russell . . . . The Gift is Rich
Collier, John . . . . Indians of the Americas
Collier, Penny and Bill. . . . . . . Along the Mt. Adams Trail
Culverall, Albert . . . . Stronghold in the Yakima
                                       Country
Curtis, Edward S. . . . . Indian Days of Long Ago
Cutler, Pollack & Munat . . . . . Our Indian Heritage
Deloria, Vine Jr. . . . . Federal Role in Indian Education
De Voto, Bernard . . . . The Course of Empire
Drury, Clifford M. . . . . Marcus Whitman, M.D.
Drury, Clifford M. . . . . Chief Lawyer and the Nez Perce
                                       Indians
Dye, Eva Emery . . . . McLoughlin and Old Oregon
Fleming, Elia B. . . . . Sketches of Early High Prairie
Fuller, George W. . . . . A History of the Pacific
                                       Northwest
Ghent, W. G. . . . . The Road to Oregon
Goddard, John . . . . The Evergreen State
Guie, H. Dean . . . . Bugles in the Valley
Gunther, Erma . . . . A Further Analysis of First
                                       Salmon Cer.
Hebard, Grace . . . . Sacajawea
Hussey, J. A. . . . . Fort Vancouver

Johnson & Gates . . . . The Empire of the Columbia
La Farge, Oliver . . . . American Indian
Lyman, William Denison. . . . . . The Columbia River
McKeown, Martha Ferguson . . Linda's Indian Home
McKeown, Martha Ferguson . . Come to Our Salmon Feast
Mirsky, Jeanette . . . . The Westward Crossings
Monaghan, J. W. Dir. . . . . Book of the American West
Montgomery, Richard . . . . The White Headed Eagle
Nuthammer, Carolyn . . . . American Indian Food and Lore
Parkman, Francis . . . . Oregon Trail
Reilander, Cliff . . . . Yakima Indian Tribe
Ruby and Brown . . . . Half Sun on the Columbia
Steiner, Stan. . . . . The New Indian
Strong, Emery . . . . Wakemap
Strong, Emery . . . . The Stone Age on the Columbia
Tobie, Harvey . . . . No Man Like Joe
Underhill, Ruth. . . . . Indians of the Pacific Northwest
Victor, Frances Fuller . . . . The River of the West
Warren, Esther . . . . The Columbia Gorge Story
Winthrop, Theodore . . . . Canoe and Saddle
Williams, John . . . . The Guardians of the Columbia
Williams, John . . . . The Mountain that was God
Wingert, Paul S. . . . . Prehistoric Sculptures of the
                                       Northwest

The Tribal Distribution in Washington General Series in
    Anthropology
Wishram Ethnography . . . U.W. Sahaptan Texts 1935 Cu Ca vol 19
    part 1
Asymposium Anthropology . . . American Indian
Readers' Digest . . . America's Fascinating Indian Heritage
Articles on Klickitats and Yakimas in IN Oregon Historical
    Quarterly.
Articles on Klickitat and Yakima Indians in Washington Historical
    Quarterly
Letters in Possession of Mrs. Selma Neils:
    Non Young, Robert Ballou, Clarence Ballou, Ruth Toomey
Interviews in Possession of Mrs. Selma Neils:
    Guy Long, Louise Spino, Skookum Wallahee, Irving Moore-
    head, Sally Wahkiacus, Cody Slakesch, Art Vause, Hazel
    Vause, Homer Mitchell, Ollie Kreps, and Jennie and Bertha
    Wright.

INDEX

223